ACKNOWLEDGMENTS

This magazine has been published by Wharncliffe History Magazines in association with Pen and Sword Military Books Limited, with the purpose of creating an awareness and an interest in the subject of military history.

For over twenty years Pen and Sword has published numerous military, naval and aviation books covering various conflicts throughout history. A vast amount of military titles have been published over the past few years, covering the personal accounts of soldiers who have taken part in many conflicts, stretching from the First World War through to the Falklands War. The books featured in this magazine are only a few titles taken from a large selection of subjects covering The Great War.

These publications would not have been possible if it had not been for the skill and dedication of the authors, who have painstakingly researched and written about these conflicts in order to bring them to light.

Only extracts have been taken from these titles to produce this magazine and much more information can be gleaned by reading the books mentioned at the end of each chapter. Pen and Sword have included more colour illustrations and images to the text in order to add more interest for the reader, making this a very special publication.

Pen and Sword Books would like to thank; Roni Wilkinson, Herbert Sulzbach, Jack Horsfall, Nigel Cave, William Langford, Matthew Richardson and Tonie and Valmai Holt, whose works have appeared in this magazine 1914 – FIRST BATTLES OF THE GREAT WAR 100 YEARS ON

Wharncliffe

HISTORY MAGAZINES

In association with;

Pen & Sword Military Books.

First published in Great Britain in 2014 by
Wharncliffe History Magazines
47 Church Street
Barnsley
South Yorkshire
S70 2AS

Copyright © Wharncliffe Publishing, 2014

Edited by Roni Wilkinson and Jonathan Wright

Design, layout & photograph colouring:
Jon Wilkinson and Mat Blurton

Maps by Dominic Allen

ISBN: 978 184884 102 4

A CIP catalogue record for this book is
available from the British Library.

Printed and bound in the United Kingdom

For a complete list of Pen & Sword titles please
contact
PEN & SWORD BOOKS LIMITED
47 Church Street, Barnsley, South Yorkshire,
S70 2AS, England
E-mail: enquiries@pen-and-sword.co.uk
Website: www.pen-and-sword.co.uk

CONTENTS

1914

INTRODUCTION

At the beginning of the twentieth century the then civilised world had everything to look forward to: the industrialisation of the previous hundred years was evolving with ever-increasing momentum promising an exciting future; electricity had been harnessed; steam-driven engines had revolutionised transport; the internal combustion engine had been invented and man had learned how to fly like the birds. Then, in the second decade, it all turned sour as countries set on each other turning the inventions of peace and promise into weaponry. The resulting conflict spawned further loathsome contrivances to destroy humanbeings, such as poison gas and flame-throwers. What had caused the change? Nationalism and patriotism whipped up by religious institutions in the countries involved must surely take the blame.

As to the mechanics of the outbreak of the Great War, historians will continue to debate and each generation of them will doubtless revise the works of those living closer to the events of 1914-1918, as they seek to throw fresh light on that terrible period in the history of the world. This magazine looks at the last five months of 1914 as the nations, one after another, tumbled into war. How did it all come about?

In his paper *J' Accuse* Dr David Miller lays the blame for the war against the German Empire at the door of the French, in particular the Parti Colonial, drawn from the most powerful politicians, diplomats, bankers, industrialists and journalists in France. In the aftermath of the Franco-Prussian War of 1870-71, the capture of Paris, defeat of the French army and the loss of Alsace-Loraine, the Parti Colonial's masters conspired for revenge.

With a succession of weak French governments in the nineteenth and twentieth centuries, the Parti Colonial was effectively more powerful than its employers in the forming of foreign policy. Certainly that was the case with the Viviani government in office in 1914. Using its powers of diplomacy and with a well-defined secret agenda the Parti Colonial succeeded in forming an alliance with Russia. Germany was thus bracketed with potentially hostile countries on two frontiers. Italy, Japan, Spain and the United States were wooed in an attempt to draw them into the French diplomatic camp. The cartoon on page 11 of this journal illustrates the results of diplomatic chicanery.

The Parti Colonial had been unwittingly aided in its machinations by German foreign policy under Kaiser Wilhelm. The clever diplomatic manoeuvring of Bismark, who had always sought to keep France isolated, had been abandoned.

With its eye on a short war the Parti Colonial worked on a domestic, nationalistic revival within France.

In the Baltic state of Serbia visiting members of the Austrian royal family, Archduke Ferdinand and his wife, were shot and killed. Austria made demands on Serbia that could not be accepted without modification. Austria declared war on Serbia. Russia mobilised in support of Serbia. Germany declared war on Russia and attacked France to knock her out in a few weeks. Following victory in the west troops would be transported to the east to defeat Russia. The German war plan included a sweep through neutral Belgium.

Great Britain declared war on Germany. '*All over by Christmas*' was the view by many in August 1914.

What was it like to be a part of a massive invading army? In the article 'War Diary of a German Artilleryman' an extract has been taken from the best-selling classic *With the German Guns* by Herbert Sultzbach. His diary covers from October to Christmas.

Already the news was grim concerning the fighting in France and Belgium: the British army was retreating before the German invader, but not before the Battle of Mons had been fought. Our extract is taken from a bestseller in the Battleground series of guide books, Mons by Jack Horsfall and WW1 series editor, Nigel Cave.

It might have ended at Christmas 1914 when the two sides stopped fighting and met up in the middle of No Man's Land for a party. The famous cartoonist Bruce Bairnsfather experienced that brief truce, before the two sides were ordered to return to killing each other. An opportunity for sanity missed.

THE TERRITORIALS 1908-1914

RAY WESTLAKE

THE TERRITORIALS 1908-1914 is a unique, comprehensive record of the part-time soldiers who made up the Territorial Force that supported the regular army in the years immediately before the outbreak of the First World War. Previously information on the history and organization of these dedicated amateur soldiers has been incomplete and scattered across many sources but now, in this invaluable work of reference, Ray Westlake provides an accessible introduction to the Territorial Force and a directory of the units raised in each county and each town.

ISBN: 9781848843608 • WAS £19.99 • **NOW £15.99**

TRACING THE RIFLE VOLUNTEERS

RAY WESTLAKE

FROM 1859 TO 1908 the Rifle Volunteers played an essential role in Britain's national defence, yet their history has been sadly neglected. Little information is available on these dedicated, amateur soldiers who were recruited into the ranks of a military organization that flourished across the country. But now, in this invaluable book, Ray Westlake, a leading authority on the military history of Victorian and Edwardian Britain, provides a concise, accessible introduction to the Rifle Volunteers and a comprehensive directory of the units raised in each county and each town.

ISBN: 9781848842113 • WAS £25.00 • **NOW £20.00**

TRACING BRITISH BATTALIONS ON THE SOMME

RAY WESTLAKE

NEARLY NINETY-EIGHT YEARS have passed since the Battle of the Somme was fought; interest in this, the bloodiest battle of the First World War, has never waned. Ray Westlake has collated all the information so painstakingly gathered, to produce a comprehensive compendium of the exact movements of every battalion involved in the battle. This book is invaluable not only to researchers but to all those visiting the battlefield and anxious to trace the movements of their forbears.

ISBN: 9781844158850 • WAS £14.99 • **NOW £11.99**

BRITISH BATTALIONS ON THE WESTERN FRONT

RAY WESTLAKE

THIS BOOK PROVIDES A UNIQUE account of the 291 infantry battalions of the British Army that served in France and Belgium from 1st January to the end of June, 1915. Over 500 volumes of war diaries and unit histories have been consulted, along with personal memoirs and diaries. Detailed records of movements, both in and out of battle areas and on a day-by-day basis, are covered in Westlake's meticulous style.

ISBN: 9780850527681 • WAS £19.95 • **NOW £15.96**

BRITISH BATTALIONS IN FRANCE AND BELGIUM 1914

RAY WESTLAKE

THE AUTHOR HAS PAINSTAKINGLY COMPILED a comprehensive compendium of the exact movements of every regiment involved on the various battlefields in France and Flanders during World War One.

ISBN: 9780850525779 • WAS £21.95 • **NOW £17.56**

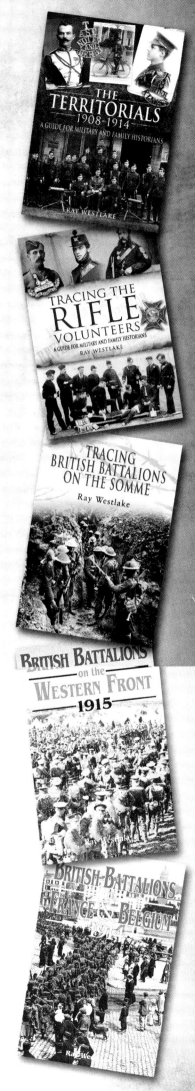

Copies of the above titles are available from all good bookshops or from the Publisher direct.
PEN AND SWORD BOOKS LTD, 47 CHURCH STREET, BARNSLEY, SOUTH YORKSHIRE, S70 2AS.

TEL: 01226 734222

VISIT: **www.pen-and-sword.co.uk**
for the latest information and offers from Pen and Sword Books Ltd.

'The driver took a wrong turn and was reversing slowly when Princip stepped forward, revolver in hand, and fired the fatal shots killing the couple. Within a short while every member the gang of assassins was arrested..'

A HURRYING TO CALAMITY – THE SPARK

The Balkans was a powder keg with its numerous small countries and its peoples speaking some fifteen plus languages; added to this were the two rival faiths of Christianity and Islam further dividing men. The bulk of the population of the Balkans professed the Greek Orthodox faith that looked longingly at Constantinople – which they regarded as their sacred city. The stage was set for the most terrible conflict the world had ever experienced, for the increased tensions in the Balkans prepared the ground for the assassination of the Austrian heir-apparent by a seventeen year old Serb student. The spark which ignited the fuse of war occured at the end of June 1914

By Roni Wilkinson

Extracted from *Pals on the Somme* and reproduced by permission of Pen & Sword Books Ltd.

Archduke Franz Ferdinand, nephew and heir to the Austro-Hungarian Emperor Franz Josef, and his wife were the victims of a Bosnia-Serb outrage while on a state visit to Sarajevo on 28 June 1914. It was strange that he should have been selected for the revolutionary gesture for he was perhaps the most liberal-minded member of the Hapsburg dynasty, often, it has been said, to his own detriment within court circles.

The Royal couple were to be driven to the Governor's residence and six members of the assassination team dispersed themselves along the route looking for opportunities to commit murder. Within minutes of the motorcade getting under way a bomb was thrown by gang member Cabrinovitch and the Archduke instinctively sought to ward it off. It struck the vehicle and bounced off to explode in the vicinity of the following car where fragments injured two Austrian officers. Immediately the wounded aides were driven to hospital. The Archduke ordered his driver to make for the same place so that he could ascertain the extent of the injuries of his staff. In the event, the driver took a wrong turn and was reversing slowly when Princip stepped forward, revolver in hand, and fired the fatal shots killing the couple. Within a short while every member the gang of assassins was arrested.

The assassinations called forth a strong note of protest and a message amounting to an ultimatum from Austria, in which they accused the Serbians of tolerating the machinations of dissident groups ranged against the Austrian-Hungarian monarchy. Although holding itself guiltless, Serbia made wide concessions. However, they

Archduke Ferdinand crown prince of Austro-Hungarian empire.

could not accede to all ten points listed in the note:

1. To suppress all publications inciting to hatred of Austria-Hungary and which were directed against her territorial integrity.

2. To dissolve forthwith the Narodna Odbrana ['National Defence' – a propaganda society formed in 1908 to present Serbia's cause to the world]; and to confiscate all its means of propaganda; to treat similarly all societies engaged propaganda against Austria-Hungary, and to prevent their revival in some other form.

The Archduke Ferdinand and his consort set out on their final journey to the town hall in Serajevo.

3. To eliminate from the Serbian educational system anything which might foment such propaganda.

4. To dismiss all officers or officials guilty of such propaganda, whose names might subsequently be communicated by Vienna.

5. To accept the 'collaboration in Serbia' of Austria-Hungarian officials in suppressing 'this subversive movement against the monarchy's territorial integrity.

6. To open a judicial inquiry into the murders, and to allow delegates of Austria-Hungary to take part in this.

7. To arrest without delay Major Tankosic and Milan Ciganovic, implicated by the Sarajevo inquiry.

8. To put an effectual stop to Serbian frontier officials sharing in the 'illicit traffic in arms and explosives', and to dismiss certain officials at Sabac and Loznica who had helped the murderers to cross over.

9. To give explanations regarding the 'unjustifiable language' used by the high Serbian officials after the murder.

10. To notify Vienna without delay of the execution of all the above measures.

Point 6 was a violation of the Serbian Constitution and their Law of Criminal Procedure and consequently the Serbian government felt unable to comply fully. It did however, agree to the other demands. More than ready to make what reconciliatory moves it could the Serbian government also stressed that it would be prepared to refer the matter to the Hague Court, should the Austro-Hungarian government feel dissatisfied.

The last thing that the government of Serbia wanted was another war, they had just been involved in two and were exhausted. It was generally agreed by the Great Powers that they were unlikely to have done anything so provocative as being a party to murdering the heir to the Hapsburg dynasty – neither instigating it nor desiring it. Even some German diplomats could not see the logic or reason in the Serbian government picking a fight with a more powerful neighbour and saw the reply to the ultimatum as compliance. Not so the Viennese government. A week after the assasination, Franz-Joseph, Emperor of Austria-Hungary, wrote to the Kaiser of Germany:

'According to all the evidence so far brought to light, the Sarajevo affair was not merely the bloody deed of a single individual, but was the result of a well-organized conspiracy, the threads of which can be traced to Belgrade and although it will probably prove impossible to get evidence of the complicity of the Serbian Government, there can be no doubt that its pol-

Cabrinovitch threw the bomb that was warded off by the Archduke.

Princip fired the fatal pistol shots. Police photograph shows signs of a beating.

icy, directed towards the unification of all countries under the Serbian flag, is responsible for such crimes, and that a continuation of such a state of affairs constitutes an enduring peril for my house and my possessions.'

As may be judged from the tone of the letter, there was absolutely nothing that the Serbian government could do to placate the Emperor and avoid war. Assurance of support for the Austrian stance came by telegram the following day from German chancellor, Herr von Bethmann-Hollweg who, speaking on behalf of Kaiser Wilhelm, wrote:

'His Majesty desires to say that he is not blind to the danger which threatens Austria-Hungary, thus the Triple Alliance as a result of the Russian and Serbian Panslavic agitation. As far as concerns Serbia, His Majesty of course cannot interfere in the dispute now going on between Austria-Hungary and that country, as it is a matter not within his competence. The Emperor Franz-Joseph may, however, rest assured that His Majesty will faithfully stand by Austria-Hungary as is required by the obligations of this alliance and of his ancient friendship.'

Germany would stand by Austria-Hungary in her punitive action against Serbia whatever the consequences.

Regarding help and support for Serbia, as it became increasingly obvious that there was no placating the

German Kaiser Wilhelm and Franz-Joseph, Emperor of Austria-Hungary, stood together against Serbia.

National alliances which ensured world war would result from any fallout: Germany and Austro-Hungary in one camp (Central Powers), ringed about by France, Russia, Great Britain (Triple Entente) and Italy.

House of Hapsburg, the Tsar of Russia sent a telegram to the prince regent of Serbia on the 24 July:

> 'When your Royal Highness applied to me at a time of special stress, you were not mistaken in the sentiments which I entertain for you, or my cordial sympathy with the Serbian people. So long as the slightest hope exists of avoiding bloodshed, all our efforts must be directed to that end; but if in spite of our earnest wish we are not successful, your Highness may rest assured that Russia will in no case disinterest herself in the fate of Serbia.'

Russia stated that her forces would be mobilized the moment Austrian troops crossed the Serbian frontier. Immediately, the attitude of Germany stiffened and it became evident that even a partial mobilization of the Russian army would be regarded as a belligerent act. These were grounds for war, not only against Russia but against Russia's ally, France. In vain Russia protested that her partial mobilization was a precautionary undertaking. Secretly, Germany's own preparations for war were well ahead of those of any other European nation, as events would soon prove.

Matters began to move quickly. Four days later, on 28 July at 11 am, Austria-Hungary declared war sending a telegram to that effect to the Serbian town of Nis. They considered it the golden opportunity to settle the matter once and for all – that troublesome hotbed of intrigue

Tsar Nicholas II of Russia.

and rebellion Serbia would be 'brought to heel'.

The arrival of the declaration that was to launch the biggest slaughter in the history of mankind was remembered by a junior official in the Serbian Ministry of Foreign Affairs, 'I was having lunch in the Hotel Europa in Nis. The dining-hall was crowded with people from Belgrade. Between twelve and one o'clock a postman entered and handed something to Mr Pasic, who was eating about two tables away from me. Pasic read what the postman had handed to him and then stood up. The room fell deadly silent and he announced "Austria has declared war on us. Our cause is just. God will help us!"' An identical telegram was sent from Vienna to the Serbian supreme command.

Doubts about the authenticity of the telegrams arose when at 3 pm Pasic enquired of the German minister only to be told that the German Legation knew nothing about the matter. Immediately Pasic sent cables to the governments in London, Paris and St Petersburg about the strange telegrams asking if it could possibly be true that Austria-Hungary had declared war on Serbia.

Before he got answers to his cables Belgrade authorities informed him that guns were bombarding the Serbian capital. The last hopes that war could be avoided vanished.

True to her word and in support of her Serbian friends, on Friday, 31 July, Russia declared war on Austria and the following day Germany retaliated by declaring war on Russia. Because of the German war plan (drawn up by German strategist Count Alfred von Schlieffen) any war with Russia on the eastern frontiers meant an attack, in the first instance, in the west against

Albert, King of the Belgians.

Germany's traditional enemy, France. The theory was that by the time Russia had effected total mobilization, the enemy on the opposite border would have been annihilated within forty-two days. The national railway system would then transport a major part of the German army eastwards to defeat, in turn, the Russians who would likely have overcome the holding forces and be threatening German territory.

The German plan also called for passage of its main thrusting columns, comprising four armies, through neutral Belgium to get at France. Britain, whose foreign policy had always been to avoid, if at all possible, a super power dominating Europe, particularly the coastline opposite her shores, sought to support Belgium. The German government, on Sunday, 2 August, had demanded that Belgium grant its armies free passage or suffer the consequences. At 10 o'clock that night German troops crossed the Belgian frontier from the direction of Aix-la-Chapelle. Simultaneously their forces entered the independent duchy of Luxemburg en route to the French border. The first shots were fired by the French outposts in the provinces of Alsace and Lorraine. On Monday Albert King of the Belgians telegraphed King George V asking for help:

> '*Remembering the numerous proofs of Your Majesty's friendship and that of your predecessor, and the friendly attitude of England in 1870 and the proof of friendship you have just given us again, I make a supreme appeal to the diplomatic intervention of Your Majesty's Government to safeguard the integrity of Belgium.*'

The British government was officially informed by Belgium on 4 August that German troops had invaded Belgium and that the violation of that country's neutrality had become an accomplished fact.

Immediately, a telegram was sent by British prime minister Mr Asquith to the British ambassador in Berlin, to the following effect:

> '*The King of the Belgians has appealed to His Britannic Majesty's government for diplomatic intervention on behalf of Belgium. The British government is also informed that the German government has delivered to the Belgian government a note proposing friendly neutrality pending a free passage of German troops through Belgium and promising to maintain the independence and integrity of the kingdom and its possessions on the conclusion of peace, threatening in case of refusal to treat Belgium as an enemy.*'

Sir Edward Grey, the British Foreign Secretary, had requested an answer within twelve hours. The Prime Minister, Mr Asquith, then read a telegram from the German foreign minister, which the German ambassador in London had sent to Sir Edward Grey. The reading was greeted with hoots of laughter in the House of Commons:

> '*Please dispel any distrust that may subsist on the part of the British government with regard*

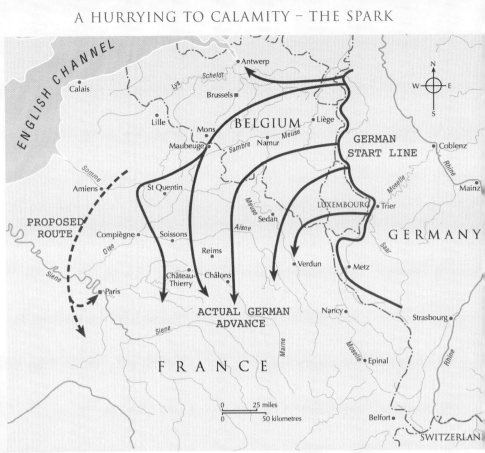

to our intentions by repeating most positively the formal assurance that even in case of armed conflict with Belgium, Germany will under no pretensions whatever annex Belgian territory.'

Premier Asquith was able to read to the House a telegram from Brussels which informed them that, the German government 'deeply to its regret', would be compelled to carry out by force of arms the measures 'considered indispensible in view of the French menace'.

Excited crowds gathered at Buckingham Palace and in Parliament Square, London, to witness the last seconds of peace ticking away and to greet a popular event. The deadline for Britain's ultimatum to Germany expired at 11 o'clock (midnight in Germany). The striking of that fateful hour by Big Ben was the signal for an almighty, enthusiastic roar. Patriotism, 1914 style, was born. Tuesday, 4 August 1914, Britain and Germany were at war.

It had come as no surprise to some. Certainly British Military Intelligence had been predicting an all-out war with Germany since 1907, according to recent research into hitherto unexamined documents originating in the Foreign Office and Admiralty. British agents had detected a pro-war faction among the senior officers of the German military who had become convinced that war was essential for the ongoing development and benefit of the German army. That belligerence was aimed mainly at Great Britain and her Empire and was, apparently, fed to the

THE GERMAN ADVANCE THROUGH BELGIUM

Kaiser as a regular diet of hate. The Kaiser, however, would make his move when he was absolutely convinced of a victory. With the situation in Serbia he felt that the opportunity had arrived. Certainly the masses were ready for it.

There were scenes of patriotic fervour and martial ardor during the first days of August in all the European capitals directly affected by the war. In London, Paris, St Petersburg, Vienna and Berlin enthusiastic crowds filled

German soldiers of the 47th Infantry Regiment advance through north eastern France, August 1914.

the streets, singing national anthems and hymns, cheering their respective rulers and national heroes. The 'War of the Ages' had been launched and, over the coming months, the citizens of those same capitals of Europe would begin to experience heart-rending mourning as husbands, sons and lovers began to fall on the battlefields in such numbers as to surpass all former records of history.

IN SUPPORT OF BELGIUM

In Britain preparations for war had been going on some days prior to the expiration of the deadline. Reservists were called up and the Territorials were brought back from their summer training. Bank Holiday weekend (Bank Holiday Monday was 3 August) was the start date for the annual army camps, however, this time, the unfolding international events were to add excitement and drama to the occasion. No sooner had the trains taken the 'Saturday Night Soldiers' to their seaside locations for their fortnight of military training than they were running them back to their towns and cities. It was no mean feat, the South Midland Division under canvas near Rhyl was estimated to number around 10,000 men. As disgruntled holiday-makers were finding their excursion trains had been cancelled, the territorials were arriving back at their drill halls. As an integral part of the National Mobilization Plan the Territorials were, within days, being transported to pre-planned coastal defence positions.

The first four infantry divisions of the Regular army, comprising two thirds of the British Expeditionary Force, were in France by 12 August shortly to be pushed back by the huge columns of grey-clad invaders. An American correspondent for the *New York World*, Alexander Powell, described the awesome spectacle presented by the invaders:

> *'It was a sight never to be forgotten. As far as the eye could see stretched solid columns of marching men, pressing westward, ever west-ward. The army was advancing in three mighty columns along three parallel roads. These dense masses of moving men in their elusive blue-grey uniforms looked for all the world like three monstrous serpents crawling across the country-side.*

> *'American flags which fluttered from our windshield proved a passport in themselves and as we approached the closed-locked ranks they parted to let us through.*

> *'We passed regiment after regiment, brigade after brigade, of infantry, and after them hus-sars, Uhlans, cuirassiers, field batteries, more infantry, more field guns, ambulances, then siege guns, each drawn by thirty horses, engineers, telephone corps, pontoon wagons, armoured motor cars, more Uhlans, the sunlight gleaming on their forest of lances, more infantry in spiked helmets, all sweeping by as irresistible as a mighty river, with their faces turned towards France.*

A fortress protecting the Belgian town of Liège smashed by German guns.

'Every contingency seems to have been foreseen. Nothing was left to chance or overlooked. Maps of Belgium, with which every soldier is provided, are the finest examples of topography I have ever seen. Every path, every farm building, every clump of trees is shown.

'At one place a huge army wagon containing a complete printing press was drawn up beside the road and a morning edition of the Deutsche Krieger Zeitung (German War News) was being printed and distributed to the passing men. It contained accounts of German victories of which I had never heard, but it seemed greatly to cheer the men.

'Field kitchens with smoke pouring from their stovepipe funnels rumbled down the lines, serving steaming soup and coffee to the marching men, who held out tin cups and had them filled without once breaking step.

'There were wagons filled with army cobblers, sitting cross-legged on the floor, who were mending soldiers' shoes just as if they were back in their little shops in the Fatherland. Other wagons, to all appearances ordinary two-wheeled farm carts, hid under their arched canvas covers machine guns which could instantly be brought into action.

'The medical corps was as magnificent as it was businesslike. It was as perfectly equipped and as efficient as a great city hospital.

'Men on bicycles with a coil of insulated wire slung between them strung a field telephone from tree to tree so the general commanding could converse with any part of the fifty mile long column.

'The whole army never sleeps. When half is resting the other half is advancing. The soldiers are treated as if they were valuable machines which must be speeded up to the highest possible efficiency. Therefore they are well fed, well shod, well clothed, and worked as a negro teamster works mules.'

The Germans had expected that Belgium, with its small army would, at most, offer a token resistance. While ineffectual in halting and throwing back the grey hordes surging across their fields and into their towns, they did manage to cause a delay of three valuable weeks. Close to the border were the Belgian towns of Visé and Verviers and they had been the first objectives of attack and Belgian defence. Both were occupied after desperate resistance and the town of Visé was systematically burnt in reprisal, it was claimed, for the firing by civilians on the German invaders.

A vivid description of the march into Belgium and the fighting in front of the fortress-ringed frontier town of Liège was given in a letter by one German officer who was wounded in the battle:

'Our trip towards the Belgian border was a triumphal procession, although it was pouring with rain as we marched through the Ardennes. The towns and villages seemed to us to be deserted. We had no rest and during the night we were fired upon.

'On 6 August, at dawn, we reached the Ourthe valley – there were obstacles everywhere. It was an awful march, the roads were frequently blocked by felled trees and rocks, and bridges over rivers had been destroyed. In the afternoon we took up quarters in a village some distance south of Liège.

'Seven o' clock in the evening the order was given by the captain to march on Liège. It seemed impossible; we felt that we could go no farther for the forts were thirty-five kilometres away. But, nevertheless, we pressed on.

'After thirty minutes the column was fired upon from the surrounding high ground. It was dark and pouring with rain and a thunderstorm was roaring. Then suddenly shots were fired from quite close by and we see some of our men falling. Then we learned that our baggage train, bringing up the rear, had been attacked. Such are the atrocities of the franc-tireurs [guerillas, or civilian snipers]. The night cleared and there was bright moonlight. In the distance we could hear the sound of heavy artillery pounding the forts.

'One Company was ordered to turn back to the village that we had just passed through. There, the people were all shot and their houses burned.

'Meanwhile we keep marching on, and close to Liège we turned off and took cover behind a wood. Four regiments lay down their knapsacks and 'iron rations' were consumed. After resting we were then roused and formed up in attack formation. The last exhortations were given.

'We charged into a hail of bullets and shells which were being fired in our general direction, but with little accuracy. Along the way we ran past our own artillery with the guns and limbers stuck up to their axles in mud.

'Suddenly a hail of bullets came at us from directly ahead. It was our own men who were firing upon us – we had been mistaken for the enemy. Just in time we were identified and the firing ceased. We were then directly in front of

'After thirty minutes the column was fired upon from the surrounding high ground. It was dark and pouring with rain and a thunderstorm was roaring.'

15

Belgian infantry, at a make-shift barricade, await the German massed columns flooding through their countryside, villages and towns.

the firing line of the forts. There was confusion all around and the password 'Woerth' was given as friend and foe looked alike.'

From the foregoing it is understandable that with hundreds of thousands of soldiers on the march cases of mistaken identity should occur. Today 'Friendly Fire' or 'Blue on Blue' (or, more commonly, 'Home Goal') are terms used to described such incidents. Back in August 1914 wounding and death suffered by the Germans in their advance was attributed to armed civilians, rather than highly nervous and trigger-happy comrades. Similarly, bridges, tunnels and telegraph lines that were blown up had to be the work of civilian saboteurs rather than Belgian military engineers.

Quaffing looted wine in order to quench their thirst during the marches probably contributed to the shooting incidents that were taking place. Again, believing such casualties to be the result of the work of Belgian civilians, the German army took reprisals. Time and again the actions of so-called *franc-tireurs* were used as the reason for the bombardment and burning of towns and villages. They were claimed by the Germans to be acts of revenge for hostile acts carried out by non-combatants and intended to prevent their occurrence elsewhere by striking terror into the hearts of the Belgian populace. Whatever the pretext or excuse, the historical fact remains that the result of the German progress toward the Franco-Belgian border constituted a martyrdom for Belgium. It gained the sympathy of the

Accused of firing on the German columns and blowing up bridges these Belgians are being marched to a place of execution.

16

German infantry come under fire somewhere in Belgium.

civilized world, put off potential allies to the Central Powers and stiffened Belgian resistance. The German timetable was thrown out enabling the French fully to mobilize and Britain to land its expeditionary force. Consequently, between them, the British and the French forces were able to effectively oppose the German advance on Paris.

It was becoming clear to the discerning leaders in the west that it would take a mighty force to halt and ultimately defeat the powerful war machine that had been fielded by the German High Command. Little wonder that the Kaiser referred to the British Expeditionary Force, which numbered in the first weeks a mere 94,000 men, as 'contemptibly little'.

ARTICLE II.

Her Majesty the Queen of the United Kingdom of Great Britain and Ireland, His Majesty the Emperor of Austria, King of Hungary and Bohemia, His Majesty the King of the French, His Majesty the King of Prussia, and His Majesty the Emperor of all the Russias, declare, that the Articles mentioned in the preceding Article, are considered as having the same force and validity as if they were textually inserted in the present Act, and that they are thus placed under the guarantee of their said Majesties.

ARTICLE VII.

Belgium, within the limits specified in Articles I., II., and IV. shall form an independent and perpetually neutral State. It shall be bound to observe such neutrality towards all other States.

PALMERSTON
British Plenipotentiary
SYLVAN VAN DE WEYER
Belgian Plenipotentiary
SENFFT
Austrian Plenipotentiary
H. SEBASTIANI
French Plenipotentiary
BÜLOW
Prussian Plenipotentiary
POZZO DI BORGO
Russian Plenipotentiary

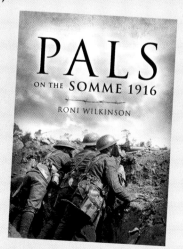

'The façade of one house collapses, mounted patrol horses tear along the streets, and the first dead and wounded are lying about. You can't see at all where the firing is coming from. I stand, or rather hang, on the reins between my two horses: No. 2 gun keeps on firing and firing.'

WAR DIARY OF A GERMAN ARTILLERYMAN

Frankfurt-am-Main, 28 June, 1914: Archduke Francis Ferdinand has been murdered, with his wife (the Duchess of Hohenberg), by two Serbs at Sarajevo. What follows from this is not clear. You feel that a stone has begun to roll downhill and that dreadful things may be in store for Europe.

By Herbert Sulzbach

Extracted from *With the German Guns* and reproduced by permission of Pen & Sword Books Ltd.

Iam proposing on 1 October to start my military service instead of going to Hamburg as a commercial trainee. I'm twenty, you see, a fine age for soldiering.

14 July: I travel to Würzburg, report to the 2nd Bavarian Field Artillery Regiment and get accepted.

Böhm, the German airman, has scored a world record with 24 hours of continuous flight.

23 July: Ultimatum delivered to Serbia by Austria-Hungary.

No strong action by Austria appeared to have been taken since the assassination on 28 June until suddenly this note was presented, containing ten demands which among other things were supposed to allow Austria herself to take action on Serbian soil against activities hostile to Austria. Serbia has to accept the ultimatum within 48 hours, otherwise Austria reserves the right to take military action. A world war is hanging by a thread.

25 July: Unbelievably large crowds are waiting outside the newspaper offices. News arrives in the evening that Serbia is rejecting the ultimatum. General excitement and enthusiasm, and all eyes turn towards Russia – is she going to support Serbia?

The days pass from 25 to 31 July. Incredibly exciting; the whole world is agog to see whether Germany is now going to mobilize. I've hardly got enough peace of mind left to go to the bank and do my trainee job. I play truant as though it were school and stand about all day outside the newspaper offices, feeling that war is inevitable.

Friday, 31 July: State of war declared and total mobilization announced in Austria-Hungary.

Saturday, 1 August: 6.30 pm: The Kaiser orders mobilization of the Army and Navy. That word 'mobilize', it's weird, you can't grasp what it means. First mobilization day is 2 August.

Try as I may I simply can't convey the splendid spirit and wild enthusiasm that has come over us all. We feel

Herbert Sulzbach.

we've been attacked, and the idea that we have to defend ourselves gives us unbelievable strength.

Russia's dirty intrigues are dragging us into this war; the Kaiser sent the Russians an ultimatum as late as 31 July. You still can't imagine what it's going to be like. Is it all real, or just a dream?

My brother-in-law travelled to Wilhelmshaven on 3 August. He's a staff medical officer on the Naval Reserve. I put my name down on the nominal roll, as a war volunteer, of course; I'm hoping to get into our 63rd. I go to the barracks and try my luck. A lot going on there, and people very enthusiastic; some tearful good-byes too, as the regiment of regulars is pulling out.

I visit my nice motherly friend Martha Dreyfus and get given a lucky penny. My brother is in London and means to be here in four days' time, or six at the most.

Berthold, who has been our manservant for quite a time, is joining his regiment, and our dear friend Hauptmann Rückward has already pulled out of barracks. Very rapidly, you might almost say in a few hours, nearly all the men one knows have disappeared from civilian life. My sister and all her married women friends are left alone – their husbands have joined the colours. The first enemy aircraft is reported to have flown over Frankfurt.

4 August: I think I'll certainly be able to get into the 63rd. All of us who have reported as war volunteers are enduring hours of anxiety in case there won't be room for us.

Mobilization is going as smoothly as you please, and people feel a terrible hatred for the Russians and the French. England's attitude is ambiguous.

Reports are coming in of the first clashes on the frontier. There's a huge spy-hunt going on inside

Germany, and notices in foreign languages are disappearing from the shops. And a curfew at 11 o'clock. My friends who have already completed their year of military service are all off now, and our beautiful Adler car has been 'called up' too.

The German Army has a huge job on its hands: war on two fronts. We can only hope that Providence will stand by us. At home our first officer is billeted on us, OW, Leutnant, Army Reserve, from Herborn.

On 4 August, in the evening, news that England has declared war.

7 August: My brother has landed at Hamburg, so he got away from England all right. My last day in civvy street. News in the evening that Liège has been taken by assault.

8 August: I am a soldier at last. Everybody so friendly, most touching. The girls are all most concerned, getting very motherly. Incidentally, I've been unbelievably lucky to have got into the 63rd, because no fewer than 1,500 war volunteers applied there in the first few days, and only 200 were taken; many of my school friends are in the same artillery battalion. My brother-in-law is in the SMS *Ariadne*.

9 August: My brother has arrived.

10 August: We are allowed out into the town in our fatigue uniforms: it is not very easy for us, since we can't even salute properly yet, but we manage it without being too glaringly conspicuous. The next few days are given over to training; the old drivers take particular pleasure in making us do 'stables', so that we get to know this aspect of military life. It isn't easy at first to muck out the stalls, water the horses, feed them and groom them. We start having instruction periods on shooting technique.

10 August: We hear about the victorious battle at Mulhouse in Alsace; also news of the battle of Lagarde. My brother has not been accepted by the Hanau Uhlans. When Liège was taken, a Zeppelin went into action giving air support for the first time.

11 August: Montenegro declares war on us, after previously declaring war on Austria-Hungary.

13 August: France and England declare war on Austria-Hungary. Japan is still keeping neutral, but seems unfortunately to have an alliance with England.

Our Zeppelin, the *Viktoria Luise*, comes over every day to do practice bombing. The German battleship *Goeben* is unfortunately stuck in the Mediterranean. Mobilization is gradually finishing off. It went marvellously. There are still a lot of military transports coming through.

20 August: Brussels has surrendered without firing a shot (Ghent did too, on 23 August). We need to occupy Belgium before we can be happy about advancing into France, because otherwise the French, whom the Belgians would certainly have let through, would have attacked us from the rear.

20-22 August: Great victorious battle in Lorraine, after which the French go into general retreat, more like a rout. Huge number of prisoners. It's the biggest battle so far, on a 300-kilometre front. The Crown Prince of Bavaria has been in command. In Paris the people seem to be very depressed.

23 August: My sister has arrived from Kissingen with her small child. My brother is with the 9th Hussars at Strasburg. Japan's ultimatum to us over Kiauchau not replied to means war with Japan as well. The few thousand Germans over there won't be a match for the superior weight of Japanese forces, but they'll fight like heroes until they are killed or taken prisoner.

Victorious action by the Crown Prince's army at Longwy.

24 August: Big victory celebration here under summer night sky.

25 August: Namur falls.

26 August: Longwy falls.

26 August: We are sworn in.

26 August: Hauptmann Rückward has been wounded and is back from the front, also Ottomar Starke and other people I know.

27 August: Our Reserve Battalion is ready to march. Wild enthusiasm.

28 August: Belgium has been completely occupied, and the French Army bulletins are beginning to admit that they are on the defensive. Big victory at St Quentin against the British and French.

29 August: Big victory against the Russians in East Prussia; General von Hindenburg in command.

Terrible news: the *Ariadne* has been sunk in a sea battle off Heligoland. And my brother-in-law was in the *Ariadne*. I was just beginning to say good-bye to my parents and my sister and, at the very same moment, my sister had news that her husband has died a hero's death: he went down with the *Ariadne*. It is nearly impossible to say good-bye to her because she finds the sight of me in uniform too painful.

Morale at the barracks is terrific, and I'd be just as happy and enthusiastic if this terrible misfortune hadn't happened to us; even the sympathetic telegram from the captain of the *Ariadne* is not able to bring us any comfort. The death of my brother-in-law is also honourably mentioned naval despatches.

The victory in East Prussia which I have already noted seems to have had a decisive effect, since the Russians who had pushed into East Prussia are pouring back in full retreat across their own border. Down in Galicia a battle is raging between Austrians and Russians.

We've been ready to march since 28 August, the very day my brother-in-law was killed in action.

1 September: we had more shooting with live ammunition at Bergen. In the evening news that 70,000 Russians have been taken prisoner in East Prussia, a huge victory, while the gigantic battle between the Austrians and the Russians seems to have ended in a draw after six days.

2 September: Reveille at 3.45 am; then a solemn church parade, and at 8 o'clock the long-awaited march-off after a bare four weeks' training. We are among the first few volunteers to reach the front. We entrained at the goods station, and I was seized by a strange feeling, a mixture of happiness, exhilaration, pride, the emotion of saying good-bye, and the consciousness of the greatness of the hour. We were three batteries, and marched in close order through the town to the cheers of the inhabitants. We travelled away through the country I love, past Boppard, Coblenz and on past all those enchanting villages and little towns along the Rhine. We were given our rations at Mehlem.

We hear that Turkey is mobilizing against Russia.

The journey continues. The horses stand quietly in their vans, and we lie between them. It is an idyllic picture; the men are cheerful. The first night, with a wonderful full moon, makes you feel a bit melancholy. You lie there in your fatigue uniform and try to sleep. Among my fellow war service volunteers are many acquaintances and friends from my schooldays. I know my Obergefreiter, he was a hairdresser. 2 September, that is the day we marched off and the anniversary of Sedan, overwhelming victory by the German Army against the French Army at Verdun. Apart from that, the Germans are only forty kilometres from Paris. If we could only be up there ourselves!

The Austrians are having another hard fight against the Russians at Lemberg.

3 September: Aachen. We got breakfast on the station. Many convoys travelling west, but strangely enough, three Army Corps as well, travelling from the west to Russia.

Last German railway station: Herbesthal. We get very ample rations, and the horses have oats, hay and straw in plenty. At Herbesthal again, more and more military trains, and I see the first trainload of prisoners, Frenchmen and Englishmen. Poor chaps, all dirty and untidy. I gave them as much to eat as I could find. At Herbesthal our convoy train stood still for hours, and fresh German convoys kept passing in both directions. We moved off towards Brussels. Our train stopped often on the way, and you saw the first ruined villages and country mansions; we saw our first carrier-pigeon in flight. During the night, a very long halt. At first it was eerie, but then we were reassured by a beautiful full moon shining down on a ruined mansion, like a scene in a fairy-tale. The men are relaxed and cheerful.

4 September: the picture changes. You see sentries everywhere, guarding railway crossings and bridges. It doesn't look so peaceful. Towards evening we get an order to stop looking out of the train and to shut the doors. Then we get an order to harness the horses in the train – not very easy for us.

5 September: at 2 am, in the fortress at Namur, taken a few days before, we moved into the Belgian Uhlans' barracks and stables. At daybreak we snatched a few hours' sleep on the straw. Next day begins with 'stables', just the same as in barracks at home. Then we can go out and look at the town, sit in the cafes and fancy ourselves!

We hear that the German cavalry is within a few kilometres of Paris.

There are a lot of German troops in the town: Stoipe Hussars, Mainz Dragoons, Hanau Uhlans. Strolling round the town, I see the first signs of artillery fire: houses in ruins and sad-faced inhabitants. The effects of bombardment made a very deep impression on us. In the town itself, all private houses have to be shut up by 9 pm. You get back at last to the habit of washing yourself properly.

We hear of fresh resounding victories in the East, and here in the West the French seem to be desperate.

German artillery column moving towards the French town of Lille in 1914.

Namur on the River Meuse.

At my barracks is a Belgian prisoner, who attacked a German officer and knocked him about and is now going to be shot tomorrow. I talk to him and feel overwhelmed by this event – having a man in front of you who is going to be executed next day.

On many doors in the town you see the proof of our troops' good nature. You are always finding messages chalked up, saying 'Be nice, chaps, and look after the people in this house', followed by the name of a unit. The days in Namur passed quickly. We had barrack duties, went outside the town to do exercises, and in our free time we could sit in cafes and restaurants; the first close friendships were struck up between comrades. The peaceful days were interrupted from time to time by air-raid warnings. On our exercises outside the town and near the forts of Namur we saw signs of serious fighting, and the terrible effects of artillery fire: houses levelled to the ground, forests mown down, barbed-wire entanglements, trenches, packs thrown away by Belgians or Germans, earth piled up by bursting shells. In the park of a beautiful château, more graves than you could count of Germans, Frenchmen, Belgians, all killed in action – war!

We keep noticing inscriptions on the doors of houses and cottages, even in the villages, 'Very nice people, please treat them kindly. Sergeant X', sometimes written in English and French as well.

We hear that Maubeuge has fallen (40,000 prisoners, including three generals).

The best hours of these days in Namur are when you are on guard duty at night. You feel your responsibility and apart from that you have peace and quiet to think, encouraged by the fabulous summer night sky. We war volunteers get high praise from our commanding officer and from Leutnant Reinhardt.

We are in a sweat to get to the front at last.

Now and then convoys of prisoners come through, and when they do I sometimes manage to talk to a prisoner and hear what he thinks. They are all glad to be coming to Germany and to have the war behind them. This is something we can't figure out. Rumours of the most nonsensical declarations of war: Some – not all, unfortunately – are untrue. I receive sad news of the deaths of many of my acquaintances and friends, especially from our sister regiment, the 81st. Who, out of all my friends and acquaintances, is going to follow them?

25 September: warning order to prepare to march. So the days at Namur are over at last, and in great excitement we saddle up, harness our horses and move off in field marching order. Off we go, passing near the battlefield of Waterloo. It's a cold night, but all the same you fall asleep from time to time on your horse. I am the middle driver on No. 2 gun.

26 September: we go through a pretty district, and hear gunfire from Antwerp way. We pass two villages, Braine-Le Comte and Enghien.

The closest friend I've made so far is Kurt Reinhardt, who is a regular officer cadet and my Leutnant's brother. As a soldier he is just as hard-working and keen as he is an intelligent and sensitive human being.

28 September: things get more exciting. We pull away from our billets in the dark and seem to have been formed into a detachment. 2,000 men are marching with us, from the 76th Rostock, the 87th Mainz *Landwehr*, Sappers and Ulm Uhlans.

One troop of my Battery, under Leutnant Reinhardt (including my own No. 2 gun), is in the lead. For the first time we move up to firing positions at a qick trot. In the excitement, doing a gallop over a trench, we broke a wheel, the No. 1 driver's horses stumbled and both mine fell over them; I was hanging between them, but it all went very smoothly, we replaced the limber and on we went. On this first advance I actually met a man I knew from Frankfurt. We fired four whole rounds, but there was no sign of the enemy. The position is getting more ticklish, and at last we seem to be coming properly into the firing line.

Again and again, when we are passing, the windmills start to turn – suspiciously; it looks as though this is a sign from mill to mill that the Germans are coming. I have no notion where the front runs or how far away our armies are.

Billeted in a tiny, poverty-stricken village – Welle.

29 September: Awful disappointment; our unit is ordered back to Namur. On the 30th, to our great joy, we are heading west once more. In our billets at Ath we have for the first time a room with a bed – unbelievable luxury, because generally you sleep on the ground or in a stable and don't wash.

1 October: We march off towards Toumai. The first section, the one containing my gun, is in the lead again today. Twelve kilometres short of Tournai our Uhlans are fired on once again; Tournai seems to be still occupied. The detachment commander is General Wahnschaffe.

At mid-day our advance party is ordered back into the Battery. At 2 o'clock we all go into position in front of Tournai. There is British artillery beyond Toumai; since we are not strong enough, we are ordered to pull back, unfortunately; and we had such an ideal position! It's boiling hot. An enemy airman is given a dose of rifle-fire by ourselves and the infantry, without success. Just this side of Leuze an unmanned locomotive was launched full steam ahead by the enemy towards our Sappers' train; we fired at the locomotive but unfortunately did not hit it. We heard later that it didn't destroy our Sappers' train because they managed to divert it to another siding.

On the march through Leuze we see many inhabitants with frightened faces. The houses have all their window-curtains drawn. The unit which last marched through Leuze seems to have been fired on by the civilian inhabitants, so we all ride through this 'pleasant' village revolver in hand. Next day I become the No. 1 driver on No. 2 gun. We pull back again and after two hours head west once more. An aircraft is sighted, but we see the Iron Crosses under his wings in time – so he's a German.

A cavalry patrol rides towards us; they are not our Uhlans, but Hussars from another unit. Six regiments are supposed to be advancing, including the 13th Hussars from Diedenhofen and artillery as well. And a whole corps is supposed to be coming up as well to support us. They seem to be preparing for a battle. One of the Hussars was wearing the Iron Cross Second Class; this was the first time I had seen it. We get back to billets in Ath for the third time. This everlasting marching to and fro appears to have the higher purpose of misleading the enemy.

Now it's October, how very different; I had thought this season would be, just a few months ago: first I wanted to take a trainee job with an export firm in Hamburg.

There seems to be an endless amount of cavalry near here.

3 October: Our section is the advance party again. Tournai has been evacuated by the enemy; we march through the town and get stared at by the inhabitants as though we were sea monsters – not very amiably.

We go into position outside the town, dig ourselves in and spend a pretty cold night in the straw beside the horses. Full moon again. While the sun is rising, the moon is sinking in the west: what a picture! The first Sunday properly in the field. At 9.20 am we cross the Franco-Belgian border. We are in France! At 1 o'clock we are in Helemmes, a suburb of Lille. No. 1 gun had just fired on a windmill, so that No. 2 gun – mine – was in front. Only twenty or thirty men of the 76th in front of us, and the main body behind.

The buglers sound 'Fix bayonets for assault'. It was incredible hearing the signal to go into action; you couldn't help thinking of the poem we had at school, *The Bugler of Vionville*. A terrible street battle began. We were right up at the front; the first barricades had been put up in front of a railway embankment, and the infantry swarmed over them all with bayonets fixed, and now a dreadful fire was directed at us, a hail of shots from every window, cellar-opening and skylight. We unlimber, firing into these narrow streets; it rumbles and crackles like hell, and we stand with our horses only ten paces behind the guns, so that it is nearly impossible to hang on to the wildly rearing animals; but hold them we must, for very soon the guns will have to be taken forward or back by these very horses. There's no

German artillery passing through a French town. Inhabitants peer at them from behind shutters and curtained windows.

German gun crew positioning a 77mm field gun.

question of retreat with our guns!

The façade of one house collapses, mounted patrol horses tear along the streets, and the first dead and wounded are lying about. You can't see at all where the firing is coming from. I stand, or rather hang, on the reins between my two horses: No. 2 gun keeps on firing and firing. Fires are starting in several places. The hellish noise makes it almost impossible to communicate with the command posts, so that our section has to beat a retreat with the infantry out of this dreadful street, and in so doing we encounter the main body, which has meanwhile also started street fighting. The jam of vehicles and men in this street is unimaginable, and in a few minutes it has accumulated to a scene of real devastation. After we had reassembled outside the town, we tried to get into Lille by another route, but were met by further fire, especially from machine guns, and had a number of wounded in the new position. We went back once more, bivouacked in a meadow and lay in the straw recuperating from our generous baptism of fire.

5 October: We move into a new position above another Lille suburb, dig the guns in and open fire. Enemy artillery fire replies, but is ineffective. As we limber up from this position we come under heavy small-arms fire; and we only manage to move to a new position by using the greatest skill and repeatedly throwing ourselves flat on the ground. The city is brought under continuous fire. Once more, we are passed by an exceptionally large quantity of German cavalry.

6 October: Spent in our bivouac and sleep between the horses. The horses have had their tack on for days; so

have we, in our peace-time uniforms! At 5 am we move into a new position and dig the guns in once more. Then we witness an unforgettable scene: one cavalry regiment after another rides past us. The 23rd and 24th Dragoons from Darmstadt, mounted chasseurs from Trier, regiments from Metz, Karlsruhe, Bruchsal, Mulhouse and Cassel; they trot past us for hours and hours; they look terrific with their lances, and you feel that something very big is going to happen. You are actually there to see military units advance and take up their appointed places, you feel that a great battle is in preparation and you are suffused with hope and excitement. I saw quite a number of people I knew among the men moving past. How strange that people should meet on this gigantic front, pretty well on the field of battle.

It is fine to have found a friend like Fähnrich (Officer Cadet) Reinhardt – he has the same views and ideas as I have; we chat as we walk together to fetch water for the horses, and as we chat we forget the war.

We also foraged on our own account and found some marvellous wine in a deserted château; but the château itself looked terrible, everything broken and smashed to pieces – the owner will never see his fine mansion again in the state in which he left it.

I make notes for my journal, lying beside the horses. You are gradually growing a beard, and you can swear and grumble like an old soldier. You still feel it is something wonderful to be one of the millions who are able to join in the fighting, and you feel it is really necessary.

A German 77mm field gun ready to open fire.

A few quiet days follow in the same position. Our first casualties, killed on 4 October, are buried. We are quite near a village bearing the pretty name of Baisieux. At night, in the open, it is getting fairly cold.

I am proud to have been praised by my Captain for my conduct on 4 October. One is only just beginning to realize now what kind of situation we were in at the street battle on 4 October: it was providential that we got out of that fearful mouse-trap; we had not expected our baptism of fire to be so thorough. The enemy had fixed it up in such a cowardly way – he didn't let us fight properly, man to man, he just fired on us out of a snug hiding-place!

10 October: The sun is out and we are just seeing to our horses, when we receive a warning order: the Wahnschaffe Detachment is to occupy the citadel of Lille, which has been evacuated by the enemy. After a six-hour ride we get to the outskirts of Lille at about 6 o' clock; the civilians greet us, outwardly polite and nervous. Strangely, the trams are running, as though there weren't any war!

We move in, and along comes a report that our Uhlans have been fired on. Two batteries move into position, and our troop is the advance party again. On into Lille in the mist and darkness; we shoot into a cul-de-sac and can't get any further. Suddenly we get the order 'About turn, march!', since once again a volley of rapid fire is opened on us with rifles and hand-grenades from all the houses, and the situation is worse because it is night; some Uhlans' horses come back riderless, and we sit hunched up on our horses, as though you wouldn't get hit so much if you were near the horse! By some miracle we get our guns out without any casualties and camp in the open. It's an icy cold night and foggy as well. The horses are kept harnessed up, as every moment we expect the enemy to make a sortie out of Lille. You couldn't think of getting any

sleep, and for the first time we are hungry. We are worried and silent; even more than on 4 October, you have the feeling that you're not going to get out of this dead end alive. Antwerp has fallen.

11 October: Today is my nephew Herbert's birthday, today he's a year old and has never consciously seen his father, who was killed in the first action at sea on 28 August – the terrible fate that has now happened to thousands!

We make our third attempt at getting into Lille and are fired on for the third time in doing so. We now discard all consideration for the inhabitants of Lille and open heavy fire on the city centre. We are not strong enough, and have to go back again; we expect reinforcements and camp near Chereng. Our morale is not good, our minds are full of the horrors of 10 October. We found a farm near by, had our first good meal and bought some wine and jam, which our comrades much appreciated. For some days we had been sleeping in a stable and had a roof over our heads, but we didn't get much sleep – along would come the well-known warning order: March for Lille! Icy cold night, dead tired, you're half asleep on foot or on your horse. At 3.30 we went into firing positions, and the sound of firing around us became louder. We had a blanket of heavy, damp fog over us.

12 October: After a disagreeable night, the stepped-up artillery attack on Lille began. You could see a huge fiery glow: Lille was burning. We hadn't intended this destruction, but after those street battles (where the heavy fire came not only from the military enemy but

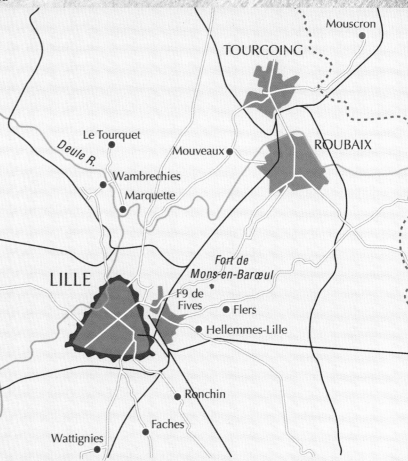

A German camera captures scenes of the fighting in Lille.

from civilians) it was unavoidable. 12 October draws to its close after we have been firing into Lille, with a few breaks, all day.

13 October: We enter Lille, our detachment from one side and part of the 19th Army Corps, which came to support us, from the other side. Now there is no more firing in the streets, and with cheerful hearts and high spirits we march in to the tune of Die Wacht am Rhein, We halt in front of the citadel; the 19th A.C. men have already brought out the prisoners, more than 4,000 French and Arabs.

Parts of Lille are still burning. More and more regiments are marching in with bands playing, and some of them march on immediately; apart from the regiments of the 19th (Saxon) Army Corps, Wiirttemberg regiments are coming through as well; and in a staff motor-car, the Crown Prince of Bavaria. At 2 o' clock we occupy the citadel, and a few French soldiers are still sitting about inside it. I have a long talk with them: we should all have been done for on 4 and 10 October if we had risked going any further into the city, and how incredibly lucky we were that they didn't spring that awful trap behind us!

The citadel itself was in an unbelievably scruffy condition; but all the same we found 500 Arab horses, rather thin, which our officers and NCOs were glad to take on. The experience of marching into the city and thinking of our own first well-fought victory gives each one of us complete satisfaction. I have another long talk with my friend Kurt Reinhardt and we get on to the subject of civilian life, talk about our childhood; all the things which you used to take for granted when they happened to you seem now idyllically beautiful. Leutnant Reinhardt has been busy all evening on a job

for the High Command, drafting a proclamation in French to the inhabitants of Lille: it is to be posted everywhere tomorrow. Leutnant Reinhardt was also commissioned to speak to the city councillors of Lille, telling them they were to comply with regulations made by the High Command and would be well treated by us provided they did so.

The French are putting the blame for not being able to hold Lille on to the British. A short while ago Lille was still not occupied by the enemy and apparently it was a British suggestion that the city was in fact put into a state of defence.

14 October: We look after our horses and have quiet duties. We are not allowed out into the town yet. The civilians are supposed to be very much embittered, all the shops are said to be closed. A number of the prisoners have not yet been evacuated, and I talk once more to some of them, also to an Englishman who gives his anger at France an airing. We hear once more from the prisoners what incredible luck we had on 4 October, since the enemy intended to let us advance right up to the citadel and then to cut off our retreat. Only the premature firing at Helemmes saved us from this fate.

14 October: A day of rejoicing, since we received our first mail—no fewer than thirty letters for me, and lovely parcels of things to eat as well.

15 October: We move from the citadel into a barracks.

16 October: Parade.

17 October: We are allowed out into the town for the first time. We ate at a restaurant on the Grande Place. The city is swarming with German military. The whole 6th Army is supposed to be gathered here. I gaze wonderstruck at many cavalry officers and other ranks all wearing the Iron Cross. The cavalry must have been doing sterling work in the last few days. You see Hussars, Dragoons, Uhlans, chasseurs and *chevaulegers*, the light cavalry. I met several school-friends; one keeps on finding it strange to meet people one knows in the middle of a war as though one were in the Goethestrasse at Frankfurt.

19 October: Warning order, but it is cancelled in the evening.

20 October: Warning order! After our few quiet days we pull out of Lille at 6 am – into another battle; we belong to the 19th Army Corps. The roads outside Lille are blocked, we only advance seven kilometres in the whole day, and go into position in a village. We meet hundreds of British prisoners-of-war being evacuated.

We belong to the 2nd Battalion, the 77th Field Artillery Regiment. The gun-limbers are standing without cover and are under constant small-arms fire.

21 October: Change of position. We pull forward, get our first glimpse of this battlefield, and have to get used to the terrible scenes and impressions: corpses, corpses and more corpses, rubble, and the remains of villages. The infantry has taken the village of Premesque by assault. The bodies of friend and foe lie tumbled together. Heavy infantry fire drives us out of the position which we had taken up, and this is added to by increasingly heavy British artillery fire. We are now in an area of meadowland, covered with dead cattle and a few surviving, ownerless cows. The ruins of the village taken by assault are still smoking. Trenches hastily dug by the British are full of bodies. We get driven out of this position as well, by infantry and artillery fire. We stand beside the guns with the horses. A dreadful night comes down on us. We have seen too many horrible things all at once, and the smell of the smoking ruins, the lowing of the deserted cattle and the rattle of machine-gun fire make a very strong impression on us, barely twenty years old as we are, but these things also harden us up for what is going to come.

We certainly did not want this war! We are only defending ourselves and our Germany against a world of enemies who have banded together against us.

22 October: British planes fly over our position and report their observations to their artillery, so that we get a thorough 'blessing'. We cook hurriedly behind some ruined houses.

We see our first air battle, the first attack by a fighter aircraft. Our battery receives its first Iron Crosses, and we feel that each individual's decoration has been given to us all.

23 October: With our support the infantry makes an assault on the British positions, but the British have dug themselves in so well that the attack does not succeed.

24 October: Hellish infantry fire, many horses wounded. Enemy fighter aircraft fly over us. Ownerless dogs have found their way to us and give us great pleasure.

Sunday, 25 October: Lovely warm autumn day. Heavy

British and French prisoners are marched through the rue Faidherbe and place du Théâtre in Lille.

artillery fire began at mid-day. We replied to it, and towards evening fetched ammunition from Lomme. Bringing up the ammunition along roads under continuous fire is very disagreeable; heavy rain and a cold autumn night: we're soaking wet and have to sleep pretty well in the water.

27 October: At 6 am we try another assault, with the infantry, on the British lines: the beggars won't give an inch, and our 109th and 138th sustain heavy casualties. We still get fired on from time to time, the shots coming from ruined houses and farms lying in some cases beyond the front, and on searching them found to our astonishment that the snipers were real heroes: wounded Englishmen.

We kill and pluck any hens still running loose and thus provide our own rations; our trusty gunners prove to be farmers and milk the ownerless cows; they don't get put

Parade in the Grande Place.

Human debris; German corpses after an attack.

off by odd shells falling near them. We construct our first crude dug-outs.

28 October: Today we have been in this position for a week. At night we came under heavy small-arms and machine-gun fire. In the meanwhile a field telephone has been laid between the individual command posts. I am a telephone operator. Of course the cable keeps getting shot through and one has to keep on patching it. The job of being a telephone operator is exceptionally interesting, since you are the man who gets first news of all important messages regarding future hostilities. The most difficult job is to keep the cable to the infantry intact. Our position lies 400 metres behind the trenches.

29 October: Fetched ammunition again. British planes drop leaflets saying that we ought to surrender. The other way round would be more sensible!

A Saxon company tries an extremely daring assault entirely on its own, which costs the lives of nearly every man in the company.

There are also quiet hours when we sit in the sun, chat and smoke and play cards. The red-letter days are always the ones when we get our mail.

We fire on enemy artillery at 2,700 metres: delayed-action fuses. Our battery has gradually gone under cover, very nicely camouflaged. Artificial trees have been planted so that the enemy airmen can't spot us. The dug-outs are like mediaeval caves.

1 November: Large-scale washing and shaving operation. We gradually notice that the static war which we have got into is becoming a permanent fixture. Rainy November days follow, all rather alike. Exchanges of fire with enemy artillery are becoming a habit. We've been in our uniforms for weeks without being able to undress. At the beginning of November we hear that Turkey has declared war on Russia – all the better for us, thank God! We get our first newspapers and read about the Emden and her heroic exploits. The first replacements for our casualties arrive. I've been sent a proper sleeping-bag from home. Now I can sleep even in the open when it's raining without getting wet!

8 November: Another red-letter day – we are kitted out in field-grey. Up to now we've been wearing our old blue peace-time uniforms.

We have to keep going out to hunt *francs-tireurs*, civilians behind the front who take every opportunity of shooting at us out of hiding-places. People have been saying for some days that America wants to declare war on Japan and Britain – if only it were true!

10 November: Dixmuiden has fallen.

11 November: Another assault is mounted against Armentières, the town in front of us. It is pouring with rain, and every inch of Armentières is burning. The battle is raging most fiercely on the right wing. Small-arms and artillery fire are going over our heads continuously. The battle doesn't slack off at night, and a cloudburst of rain and stormy wind help to make a proper Shakespeare night of it all; the limbers are brought somewhat further back, after weeks positioned right behind the guns, with the horses standing day and night in harness; the good-natured beasts are to be taken to stables in a little village, one kilometre to the rear. The poor creatures badly need a rest.

So now the limbers are at Perenchy, in a flax-spinning factory. I am here for a few days, and in the evenings drive up to the guns with mail and rations. This is generally a frightful drive through pitch darkness made even more dreadful by the fires in burning Armentières.

I'm just managing to write to my family. It is a relief to be able to report your experiences in detail. You also get time to think about beautiful things from the past, but you don't have thoughts about the future. My friendship with Kurt Reinhardt fills me with complete happiness. We see less of each other because he has had to stay with the guns.

25 November: The first snow is falling; icy wind and stormy weather. On 18 November comes the shattering news that the Emden has been sunk in Chinese waters, after very many heroic exploits which have been acknowledged with honour even by our enemies. They say the crew has been saved.

We hear that a great sea battle has been fought off Chile, ending in a victory for the German squadron. Another 20,000 Russians have been taken prisoner in the East.

The snow is covering the ground now and has turned the plains of Flanders into a winter landscape.

29 November: Mail arrives in the evening, and among other things I get a parcel as a present from my old school. Then we read the newspapers out loud to each other. At the battery meanwhile they have made themselves much more cosy. The dug-outs have tables and stoves and one even has a piano in it. Now we have been a whole month in this position. We exchange greetings with the British every day in the shape of shells; everything is gradually becoming a habit. Great

excitement and interest as we watch air fights between German and British flying men. Now and again we use our guns to attempt to knock down an enemy plane, but each time it remains an attempt. It is still a winter landscape with cloudless days, cold and sunny.

A piece of special praise from my extremely strict Feldwebel nearly fills me with delusions of grandeur. I have taken on one of the ownerless dogs. A small mongrel terrier bitch. It is very touching, by the way, how fond all our men are of animals; it indicates a good character. It's very moving to see how our old driver Strobel can never go to sleep without his little dog, and looks for him for hours if he isn't there.

We are preparing more and more for a static campaign. The infantry positions have been surrounded with strong barbed-wire entanglements.

The sea battle which I mentioned on 18 November was the battle of Coronel.

27 November: Report that another 129,000 Russians have been taken prisoner in the East. Bravo Hindenburg! We keep hearing of more heroic exploits by the *Emden*, which was sunk in such a famous action, and now further stories about the *Karlsruhe*.

Really marvellous food parcels come up in the mail, and the whole battery enjoy them.

1 December: I get leave to spend a day in Lille with two friends. Can you people at home imagine how we felt to get out of the mud of battle into a town actually inhabited by civilians and looking almost like peacetime? Shops, restaurants, cafés, civilians and military in clean clothes. We gorge our selves at the Café Mert, but at the

Another French town burns.

same time we can't avoid seeing how wretched and impoverished many French civilians look and how grieved they must be feeling. On the way back we also sat in a bar at Lomme, where we met several chaps from the 107th. They sang patriotic songs of home, but also some sentimental ones. Tomorrow they have to go back and lie in a trench: here they forget the situation and also the fact that tomorrow they may be dead.

In the evening we are back in the battery. The next few days passed monotonously, until we got a warning order on

9 December: It is very difficult to bring the guns back over this completely flat Flemish country without incurring any casualties, and actually the job ought to go to drivers of long experience, but since I am the only war volunteer, I am entrusted with the responsibility of being No. 1 driver. It is a pitch-black night and foggy as well, a difficult run, but we manage it.

10 December: At 7 am off to Lomme, where our whole Wahnschaffe Detachment assembles; we make our way through Lille and Marcq-en-Baroeuil and move into quarters in a brewery. The other ranks get private billets, we are put up by pleasant people.

11 December: Rest day.

12 December: We march to La Madeleine and entrain there – done very quickly; before that there were another four sacks of mail.

My 'pure-bred' terrier is still with me. We are given our evening rations at Hirson, and sleep in fours with the horses in the waggons.

We aren't clear yet whether we're on our way to Russia or going across to the Champagne country.

13 December: We detrain at 6.30. It's as black as night, we

Leutnant Kurt Reinhardt.

Lille station and rue de Tournai during the German occupation. The trams kept running during the fighting to capture the town.

have to saddle and bridle the horses in the dark; then we stop at a main road, we're between Rheims and Verdun. We go into quarters in Pont-Faverger, a pretty little village; the horses have good stables, and we have straw to sleep on beside the horses. We had hardly unpacked when splendid military music drew us out into the market-place, where we were surprised to see a number of senior officers strolling about, listening to the music: they gave us a really good selection. La Boheme, then folk-songs and waltzes. Then a new infantry regiment marched past with its band playing. We are just a few kilometres behind the front here, and apparently at the front itself troops are being moved about a lot. We belong to the 6th Silesian Army Corps. We see to our horses and groom them, and watch our airmen flying up to the front to reconnoitre. Pont-Faverger is in a charming position, surrounded by woods and undulating fields, and a little river flows through the centre of the village.

I spend the first evening with Kurt Reinhardt. We turn in beside the No.1 gun horses, and before we go to sleep we tell each other all the things we have been thinking about.

Kurt's father has been given the Iron Cross First Class. Kurt is as pleased about it as if he had had the medal himself. Before turning in we go and have another Bavarian beer at the Uhlans' canteen.

14 December: Duties. Then we have time to go for a walk through the village. The sun is out, really rather like spring, and I sit with Kurt Reinhardt in a garden with the little river flowing past and beside us two beautifully kept graves, belonging to men killed in action at the time when Pont-Faverger was still in the fighting line instead of being behind the front as it is today.

The next few days pass at an even pace, almost peacefully, and we can do with the rest after the strain of our exertions in Flanders in October and November.

17 December: Parade taken by General von Pritzelwitz. News of further large-scale victories against the Russians.

20 December: It is *Golden Sunday*, the last Sunday before Christmas Eve! God, what memories from peacetime! You feel that peace is something which ceased to exist ages back and that war is mankind's permanent situation. The first Christmas parcels are arriving.

21 December: Warning order – what's going to happen to all the lovely parcels? However, the order gets turned off again, so we are able to enjoy our parcels. Meanwhile, nearly everybody has got hold of a mouth-organ, and we put on a splendid concert without a brass band or anything. The CO of the 51st, who are here too, is very jolly with his men, a real charmer. Some of my mates have got cameras too, and people are busy taking snapshots.

In the evening we organize a serenade for Reinhardt, as it's his birthday: the music rings out under the bright moonlit sky. Another warning order at 10 pm. It doesn't look as though we'll be staying here much longer.

The next few days before Christmas bring us more mail and such a lot of food parcels that we can't possibly eat everything. People at home must think we're about to die of starvation.

23 December: We're getting in the mood for Christmas and go and fetch trees out of the woods. We feel well and happy. Our No. 3 and No. 4 guns leave us to become what they call Anti-Balloon Guns.

In the evening we get the shattering news that after many victories at sea, the *Graf Spee* squadron has been out-gunned by the British and sunk off the Falkland Islands: all those cruisers – *Gneisenau*, *Scharnhorst*, *Nürnberg* and *Breslau*.

24 December: It's snowing, a proper Christmas atmosphere. We are given inoculations, and at 5 there's a church parade; a big garage has been transformed into a church. On each side of the altar a fine Christmas tree is bright with candles, and 'palms' have been put up all round the walls. The officers sat at the front, with the choir on the left, and the men standing behind. It was all so solemn and uplifting that you had tears in your eyes even before you heard the strains of *Silent Night*. We were all much moved and felt quite melancholy, each of us taken up with his own thoughts of home.

Then our battery celebrated Christmas in our own back yard, under a splendid tree of our own – it was a Christmas Eve worthy of the name, and very beautiful too. The Regiment gave me a most splendid Christmas present: I was promoted to the rank of *Gefreiter*, (lance-bombardier) and it did me good to be picked out like this after so short a time.

25 December: Christmas celebrations are over. At 10 o'clock we get a warning order to march off immediately. We entrain and proceed to Challerange under a bright moonlit night, icy cold and sparkling with stars, and on to Montois, where we go into billets.

26 December: We move off again, this time through Ardeuil to Ripont. Here we are in the middle of the district whose name you know so well: Champagne! From Ripont we have to go up steep slopes over hard-frozen ground to our new firing position, which we move into at 6 o'clock. And that's our Boxing Day, our 'second Christmas Day'. The limbers stand out in the open, in the icy cold night, and we stand beside the horses, but relieve each other to get warm in the dug-outs belonging to the 16th, to whose 2nd Battalion we now belong (8th Reserve Army Corps). Christmas, 1914, is over.

The horses are withdrawn to Ripont Mill, then to another position; it's thawing now and is cold and wet as well, we are sleeping in holes in the ground and the horses are standing up to their knees in mud. Every scrap of woodland looks like a Red Indian village. Cave after home-made cave, and rough stalls, hastily knocked together, for the horses; the limbers, with the horses beside them, wait quite close to the guns as they fire. It seems even more disagreeable here than it was at Armentieres. The weather and the Champagne mud reduce our morale. There are exchanges of artillery fire which do not involve casualties.

29 December: I am given orders to ride to St Morel with Lance-Sergeant Debler. I take Lance-Sergeant Lauer's

Christmas 1914.

horse and we ride off on the two little Arabs, across fields to Granddeuil. Nothing but mud. Lance-Sergeant Debler had business with the Captain, while I waited outside. We made our way back as night was falling, and it was very hard indeed to find one's way.

In the evening I was on guard duty.

We receive our first mail in this position – that is, we have to fetch it ourselves from the rear by limber, which is a dreadfully difficult operation, with the vehicle and horses practically sunk in the mud. After these few days we really look like pigs. The fire gets heavier, it's developing into an artillery battle, what they call a 'gunners' duel'.

31 December: So 1914 is winding up today. A year to raise your spirits, but also a year of pain and sorrow, not only for us but for the whole of what is called the civilized world. This terrible war goes on and on, and whereas you thought at the start that it would be over in a few weeks, there is now no end in sight. Your feelings harden, you become increasingly indifferent, you don't think about the next day any more. It's my sister's birthday today: how will she be feeling without her husband?

A wish for us all for 1915: may this new year make up for 1914 and bring us peace. We drank the New Year in: there was no firing, we felt happy and for a few hours were able to forget the present.

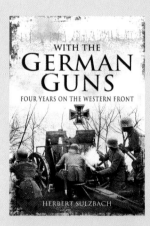

TEENAGE TOMMY – RICHARD VAN EMDEN

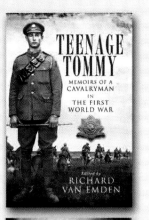

Benjamin Clouting was just sixteen years old when he embarked with the British Expeditionary Force for France in August 1914. The youngest man in the 4th Dragoon Guards, he took part in the BEF's celebrated first action at Casteau on August 22nd, and, two days later, had his horse shot from under him during the famous cavalry charge at Audregnies. Ben served on the Western Front during every major engagement of the war except Loos, was wounded twice, and in 1919 went with the Army of Occupation to Cologne. Ben's lively sense of humour and healthy disrespect for petty restrictions make *Teenage Tommy* more than just a memoir about trench warfare. It is an entertaining and moving story of life at the front.

WAS £19.99 • NOW £15.99

BRITAIN'S LAST TOMMIES – RICHARD VAN EMDEN

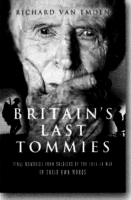

Britain's Last Tommies is a culmination of twenty years of work by Richard who has carefully interviewed and recorded the memories of over 270 veterans for this book. It is an extraordinary collection of stories told by the veterans themselves and through the author's memories of them. Their reflections are remarkable, sad, funny and moving. *Britain's Last Tommies* features an outstanding collection of old photographs taken of veterans as soldiers during the war and images of them taken in recent times in their homes and back on the Western Front, at the final veterans' reunion. *Britain's Last Tommies* offers a unique list of veterans, all of whom individually hold the poignant title of being the last Gallipoli veteran, the last Royal Flying Corps veteran, the last Distinguished Conduct Medal holder, the last cavalryman, the last Prisoner of War.

£19.99

FAMOUS – RICHARD VAN EMDEN

Famous tells the Great War stories of twenty of Britain's most respected, best known and even notorious celebrities. The generation that grew up in the late 19th century enlisted enthusiastically in the defence of the country. Many would become household names such as Basil Rathbone – the definitive Sherlock Holmes, AA Milne – creator of *Winnie the Pooh*, and Arnold Ridley who found fame and public affection as the gentle and genial Godfrey in *Dad's Army*. Each story will be examined in detail with pictures taken of the very spot where the action took place along with maps of the area that will guide enterprising readers to walk in the footsteps of their heroes.

WAS £25.00 • NOW £20.00

VETERANS – RICHARD VAN EMDEN

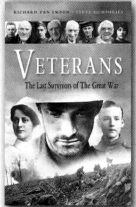

Using the veterans' own words and photographs, this book brings to life a mixture of their excitement of embarkation for France, their unbound optimism and courage, the agony of the trenches, and numbing fear of going over the top. The fight for survival, the long ordeal of those who were wounded and the ever present grief caused by appalling loss and waste of life make for compelling reading. The veterans give us first hand accounts of stark honesty, as they describe experiences that have lived with them for over 80 years.

WAS £9.99 • NOW £7.99

PRISONERS OF THE KAISER – RICHARD VAN EMDEN

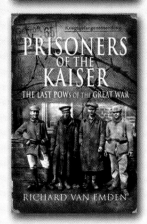

Drawing on the memories of the last surviving prisoners of the 1914-1918 war, this book tells the dramatic story of life as a POW in Germany. Stories include the shock of capture on the Western Front, to the grind of daily life in imprisonment in Germany. Veterans recall work in salt mines, escape attempts, as well as the torture of starvation and the relief at their eventual release. Vivid stories are told using over 200 photographs and illustrations, almost all of which have never before been published.

WAS £9.99 • NOW £7.99

'Sergeant Panter suddenly saw a column of German infantry entering the main street in front of them, four abreast, and proceeding as if unaware of the British presence. Within minutes the fire of him and his men had scattered the enemy, leaving many dead and wounded lying in the street.'

CONTEMPTIBLES AT MONS – 1914

It was agreed that a British force, should war be declared, would be known as the British Expeditionary Force and would take its place on the French left and these troops would concentrate at Maubeuge. The British began arriving on 22 August 1914.

By Jack Horsfall & Nigel Cave

Extracted from *Mons – 1914* and reproduced by permission of Pen & Sword Books Ltd.

Part of Brigadier General Doran's 8 Brigade (3rd Division) entered Mons itself and then moved on, 4/Middx (Middlesex) on the right, on the west bank of the Canal du Centre, whilst the other three battalions were close behind. 4/RF (Royal Fusiliers), of Brigadier General Shaw's 9 Brigade went through the town to the village of Nimy, which lay a mile to the north but was situated on the south bank of the Canal du Centre as it curved around to the south west. The three other battalions of the Brigade took up position to the west and south of the Condé Canal, which put them to the left rear of the Fusiliers.

Behind both brigades was Brigadier General McCracken's 7 Brigade; the 3rd Division was ready to move forward.

Major General Fergusson's 5th Division was spread out to the left of the 3rd, along the south bank of the remarkably straight Condé Canal. On the right was Brigadier General Cuthbert's 13 Brigade; Brigadier General Count von Gleichen's 15 Brigade in reserve and Brigadier General Rolt's 14th on the left, at its extremity

some nine miles from Mons. By the evening the troops had all found billets in factories, schools and houses; and although they only anticipated staying until the following day, they dug in, helped by enthusiastic young Belgians. Similar scenes were taking place on I Corps front, off to the right. Intermingled amongst the infantry corps were elements of Allenby's Cavalry Division, which had already got reconnaissance patrols on the far side of the canals. They were checking the way for the next move, which was to be an advance by II Corps to the north.

The 72 batteries of artillery had also been busily engaged in finding suitable positions, far from easy in the crowded country with its numerous mining villages. The majority had to be content with sites too far away from the canals to be effective, but a few did manage to get well forward. XL Brigade RFA managed to establish itself on the dominating hill a mile from Mons; 107 Field Battery established itself between the town and Nimy.

It was in the 5th Division area that there were the greatest problems. Major CS Holland, commanding 120 Field Battery of XXVII Brigade, managed to bring his four 18 pounders onto the canal towpath at Saint Ghislain.

Some of the Forward Observation Officers (FOO) thought they had found ideal places from which to view the enemy – when and if they came – from the top of the slag heaps. On the other hand, they were quick to discover the drawbacks: they were hot and smoking, with a thin crust that could break and through which a man could fall. Men from the coal mining areas were all too aware of this danger. Still, they were not going to be there for long.

The Royal Engineers were busy as well, examining the bridges to look at their load bearing capabilities and also how they might be destroyed if necessary. The CRE (Commander, Royal Engineers) of the two corps also discussed the recruiting of gangs of civilians to dig defences – in the light of what was soon to come they would be useful.

Early on the morning of 22 August Brigadier General de Lisle's 2 (Cavalry) Brigade had been out covering the approaches from Brussels, well to the front of the main bulk of the army. Major Tom Bridges (eventually to

British soldiers on the move to meet the German forces.

become a major general), commanding C Squadron of 4/(Royal Irish) Dragoon Guards, had his men in a wood just over the bridges at Nimy, about two miles up the road to Brussels. This was in the village of Casteau, about four miles from Soignies, further up on the road to Brussels. At about 7 am he saw four German cavalrymen trotting towards him. He would find out later that they were of the 4/Cuirassiers (Lancers) of the 9th (Cavalry) Division. They must have suspected something and began to turn back towards Soignies. Captain Hornby, followed by his Troop, gave chase along the paved road, alongside which a tram track ran. Corporal Thomas after a few moments dismounted and fired his rifle, hitting one of them. The pursuit continued for about a mile until, at a minor crossroads known as the Queen of Hungary, the enemy received reinforcements and a hand to hand battle of the thirty or forty cavalrymen took place. Some of the Cuirassiers were killed and a number captured – the Germans broke off the engagement and galloped off down the road.

Thomas was a regular soldier who had joined the army when he was fourteen; it is claimed that he was the first man to fire a shot in anger in the British army in the war. Hornby was awarded the DSO for his part in the skirmish. His men brought back a number of lances, helmets and other trophies; more importantly they had discovered the fact that the German cavalry were not up to their standard and that more significant numbers of Germans must be close by.

The German cavalry of the IIIrd and IXth Corps were engaged in scouting in front of the main bodies of their infantry, blissfully unaware of where the British actually were – an ignorance shared by their Army commander, von Kluck. This ignorance, and his concern about the vulnerability of his right flank, was to play an important part in the development of the Battle of Mons. At one stage he was convinced that large numbers of British troops were detraining at Tournai, well to the west, and this was to hold up the advance of vital elements of his army for several hours before it was ascertained that these troops were in fact only a brigade of French Territorials.

THE FIRST BRITISH OFFICERS TO BE KILLED IN ACTION IN THE FIRST WORLD WAR

On 16 August the Headquarters of the RFC moved from Amiens to Maubeuge. It took the army a few days to catch up with them. An officer commented;

'We were rather sorry that they had come, because up till that moment we had only been fired on by the French whenever we flew. Now we were fired on by the French and the English... To this day I can remember the roar of musketry that greeted two of our machines as they left the aerodrome and crossed the main Maubeuge – Mons road, along which a British column was proceeding.'

To safeguard against this happening again, everyone worked through the night to decorate the underside of the lower planes of all the machines with a Union Jack in the shape of a shield.

The first aerial reconnaissance by the RFC took place on 19 August; on 22 August Sergeant-Major Jillings, an observer in No. 2 Squadron, was wounded in the leg by a rifle bullet whilst flying over Maffle, south east of Ath. On the same day the first British aircraft lost to enemy fire came down. This was an Avro of No. 5 Squadron, manned by Lieutenants V Waterfall (pilot) and CGG Bayly (observer). At this stage all pilots were seconded from regiments within the army; Waterfall was in the East Yorks and Bayly was a sapper. The plane was shot down, sometime around midday, by rifle fire, quite likely by men of Walter Bloem's B Company, 12th Regiment of the Brandenburg Grenadiers.

'Suddenly an aeroplane appeared overhead. This time there was no doubt about it: the red, white and blue rings under the wings could be seen with the naked eye. I told off two groups to fire at it, and soon everyone seemed to be firing at

it. It turned back as if to return southward but too late; its nose turned down, it made several corkscrew turns, and then fell like a stone a mile or so away. Murmurs of satisfaction all round. A little later three Hussars came past and shouted out that they had found the aeroplane in a field further on. 'What about the pilot and observer', I asked. 'Both in bits, sir.'

The plane came down to earth at the village of Marcq, a mile or so away; and a Belgian peasant managed to spirit away the observer's report before the Germans arrived. This made its way, finally, to the War Office after hostilities had ended. The Germans buried the officers in the Louviau family's plot in the cemetery of Labliau at Marcq; after the war (in 1924) their remains were translated to Tournai Communal Cemetery Allied Extension. They were the first British officers to be killed in action in the First World War.

Remains of a British RFC aircraft brought down behind the German lines.

A Squadron of 19/Hussars, commanded by Major Parsons, accompanied by Captain JC Burnett and his 5th Cyclist Company (5th Division), were patrolling five miles north of the Condé Canal in the wooded area north of the village of Hautrage in front of 14 Brigade, when they met up with German cavalry. The engagement between the two small forces went on for most of the day. The Hussars were reluctant to retire as their Short Magazine Lee Enfield, with its long range, was causing so much damage; but the Cuirassiers received reinforcements. The Hussars' efforts to prevent the enemy reaching the outposts of 1/DCLI (Duke of Cornwall's Light Infantry), who only arrived at the canal in the afternoon, were gradually being overcome. They retired to Pommeroeul and then Le Petit Crepin; with the assistance of a troop of Life Guards from 4 (Cavalry) Brigade they came back over the canal.

Over on the right flank, in front of 4/Middx at the Canal du Centre, German cavalry were active in the late afternoon. They exchanged rifle fire with D Company from over the canal at Obourg. There were no casualties, but the Battalion was the first infantry to fire at the Germans in the Great War.

Very early on Saturday morning, 22 August, Field Marshal Sir John French set out by car from his Headquarters at Le Cateau to visit General Charles Lanrezac, commanding the French Fifth Army, the left of the French army, at his Headquarters near Phillipeville some sixty miles away. Utterly fortuitously he came across Lieutenant Edward Spears, who was the liaison officer between the two Armies. Spears informed French that the Germans had broken through on the River Sambre, the French Xth Corps was falling back, the German First Army was extending out to the west and that the French Fifth Army was not advancing. French returned to Le Cateau, seeing little point in going to Lanrezac's Headquarters, especially as the latter was away examining advanced posts. A more serious reason was that the two did not get on at all well, largely a consequence of Lanrezac's singularly off-hand and rather insulting manner.

Spears returned to Fifth Army Headquarters to learn further disquieting news. The German XIIth (Saxon) Corps was advancing so vigorously that it posed the threat of cutting off Lanrezac's Army; he decided that he must continue his retreat. This would expose the British army's right flank, creating a gap of some nine miles between Haig's I Corps and the Fifth Army. Spears immediately set off along the congested roads, filled with refugees and French military all heading westwards. He reported to French who had also heard from one of Lanrezac's staff officers that his Army would not be advancing and was, in fact, contemplating withdrawal. However, he requested that the BEF attack as originally planned. French realised the impossibility of this request but bravely offered to hold a line at Mons and along the Condé Canal for twenty-four hours, well aware of the consequences if Lanrezac's front collapsed.

The Headquarters of II Corps was in the small, white Chateau de la Haie, in the hamlet of Sars-la-Bruyere,

seven miles south of Mons, off the main road and without any telephone communication; it was about half way to Bavai, where French had his Advanced Headquarters. It was not a good choice of location, difficult to find in the dark and to communicate with at any time, and this was to cause Smith-Dorrien problems in due course.

At 5 am on Sunday 23 August French drove there to hold a meeting with his two Corps commanders and Allenby, who had already brought his Division back over the canal in the face of heavy German pressure. The Field-Marshal's orders were ambivalent: because of doubts about the intentions of the French they must stay where they were, prepared for any kind of move. Aircraft patrols had already started that morning and reports were awaited on the results of their reconnaissance. The BEF's Chief of Staff, Lieutenant General Sir Archibald Murray, was to remain at II Corps Headquarters, to react to whatever situation arose whilst French set off to Valenciennes. He wanted to find out what the French were doing to secure the allies left flank and to see Brigadier General Drummond, commanding the hastily formed (on 22 August) 19 Brigade. Its composite battalions had formed the Lines of Communication Defence troops. Drummond was to be warned that he might be needed to support the left flank, and that he was to come under Allenby's command, whose Headquarters were in Quievrain.

Whilst this conference was taking place the battalions of the 3rd and 5th Divisions were prepared for an attack. The attack would be made by three German corps, from right to left the IXth, IIIrd and IVth of Kluck's First Army. To his left was the Second Army, commanded by von Bülow; at this stage in the campaign, von Kluck answered to von Bülow, which provided potential for considerable friction. Von Bülow's Army lay directly in front of Lieutenant General Haig's I Corps which would not be attacked: there was concern about Lanrezac's Fifth Army and it would also hold Haig in position so that von Kluck's right hook could 'put him in the bag'. The German First Army would fall like a scythe on the British, pivoting somewhere from the north of Charleroi.

Von Kluck was not happy with the deviation from the Schlieffen Plan, feeling that he should be kept well out to the west and leaving the BEF to von Bülow and the Third (Saxon) Army. But von Kluck could only be angry and frustrated, as von Bülow controlled all three armies. The decision by the Germans would be a fateful one; whilst the BEF performed outstandingly in the battle to come.

Two other factors, with origins buried in the past, were to help the defenders. The German army adopted a policy of attacking en masse – just as the French did – advancing shoulder to shoulder in solid blocks of companies and carrying their rifles at the trail; on approaching the enemy they would fire from the hip, regardless of finding a target or taking aim. This would have an overwhelming and terrifying effect on the enemy whilst boosting their own courage. It had worked thus far (though there had been some local difficulty at Liège). The second factor was, at least in part, the consequence of Treasury miserliness over the matter of machine guns. Haig had been Director of Military Training when, in 1908, it was laid down that the infantry should be able to fire fifteen aimed rounds a minute in order to qualify for an extra payment. This would be stopped if a man did not maintain that standard. Many were able to fire even more quickly. This skill at arms was to be crucial. The army was also trained to march long distances – fifteen miles in full kit in what became known as 'Kitchener's Test'. This, too, was to be an important attribute over the next momentous three weeks or so.

SUNDAY 23RD: THE MORNING

6AM – 8AM: THE SCYTHE STARTS TO SWING

THE 3RD DIVISION.

During the evening of the 22nd Lieutenant-Colonel Hull had placed his 4/Middx in the positions where they would begin the battle the following day. His task was to hold the south bank of the Canal du Centre, facing Obourg on the hill in front of him, on the far side of the sixty-foot wide canal. There were three bridges that concerned him: on his extreme right flank at Lock No. 4; the road bridge to Obourg some five hundred yards towards his centre; and Lock No. 5, two thousand yards to the left of that. There was a further bridge, a couple of thousand yards to the north west of Lock No. 5, which was at the junction of his left flank and 4/RF.

Immediately to the right of the Obourg road bridge was the railway station, on the south bank. D Company, commanded by Captain HEL Glass, would cover both

this bridge and that at Lock No. 4 – and for a thousand yards to the north west of the bridge, an impossibly long front. Lieutenant William Allinson was in command at the station, which had been extensively strengthened by the defenders.

To the left of D Company was B Company, under the command of Major WHC Davy, who was in touch with Captain Ashburner's C Company (4/RF) at the Bridge des Bragnons.

In reserve, C Company of 4/Middx (Captain Oliver) was a thousand yards behind D, in front of a large hospital and convent, and A Company (Major WH Abell) was on its left. Lieutenant LF Sloane-Stanley, the machine-gun officer, had his two guns between them at the junction of two small roads, looking towards the woods sloping down to the south bank of the canal. Battalion Headquarters was first put into a quarry to the left of the large cemetery which was on the side of a small hill, but then moved 500 yards north west of the cemetery into the cellars of a small house on the road to Nimy.

At dawn a mist hung over the canal and light rain was falling. Shelling of the Battalion's positions had not yet started, but at 8 am the first shots of the battle came across the canal, fired at D Company positions at the station by the German 31st Infantry Regiment. They hit Private J Parr, whom many consider to be the first infantryman to be killed in the Great War. Lieutenant-Colonel Hull had, earlier that morning, told his officers that there would be no advance over the canal, saying, *'This, gentlemen, is where we will stand and fight!'.*

Lieutenant Colonel NR McMahon, commanding 4/RF, was at Nimy, on the right flank of 9 Brigade. He

A Company, 4th Royal Fusiliers, resting in the square at Mons, 22 August 1914. They were to move up to the canal bank at Nimy.

Lock 4, guarded by Captain Glass's D Company.

commanded 26 officers and 983 other ranks, of whom 734 were called up reservists. Opposite his Battalion were troops of the German IXth Corps, two regiments (ie six battalions) of the 18th Division whose attack line stretched eastwards along the Canal du Centre to D Company's (4/Middx) position. Thus there were approximately six thousand Germans against two thousand, separated by the width of the canal. The Fusiliers had six bridges to defend: from the right there was the 'joint' one held with the Middlesex; the road bridge at Nimy and the railway bridge two hundred yards to its left; the bridge at Lock No. 6, a thousand yards further left beyond the canal bend; and the Ghlin road and adjacent railway bridges five hundred yards further along the canal, the western entry to Mons.

Captain Forester held the road bridge at Nimy, which had been swung back, with two platoons whilst two other platoons were entrenched at the railway bridge and the canal bank to its left. Lieutenant Maurice James Dease, the machine-gun officer, had placed his two guns at the railway bridge, one at each side, in small emplacements of sandbags built onto the stone buttresses, with fields of fire across the canal. B

Private A F Carter. D Company, 4th Middlesex.

Company was at Nimy Railway Station with Battalion Headquarters. D Company was at Lock No. 6 and the road and rail bridges on the Ghlin road. Part of the Company was on the western side of the canal, for about a thousand yards, on flat land dominated by a large wood. A Company, under Captain Cole, was in reserve on the northern edge of Mons. In fact, only two companies, C and D, were on the defensive against the six German battalions. Captain Byng of D Company had blocked the railway bridge with large drums of cable, wheeling them into position and turning them on their side, thereby forming a barricade.

Four 18 pdrs of 107 Battery of XXIII Brigade RFA had found positions close to the station at Mons from where they could support the two companies. At 8am all was still almost quiet, although movement could be heard in the woods on the other side of the canal.

To the left of the Royal Fusiliers was 1/RSF (Royal Scots Fusiliers), who had been brought by their commanding officer, Lieutenant Colonel Douglas Smith, to the eastern end of the Condé Canal on the 22nd. He marched them over the bridge at Jemappes,

Lieutenant Holt's bridge on the Rue des Bragnons. The lifting gear is on the Maisieres side.

German lancers watering their horses.

along the pavéd road across the flat, marshy land to Ghlin, two miles away. This was his allotted position, on the left of the Londoners, for the Corps advance.

However, long before nightfall, he was withdrawn to take up positions on a two thousand yard length of the canal, from Loch No. 1 on the right to the iron lifting bridge, Pont Richebe, at Jemappes on the Battalion's left flank. Several hundred yards east of that bridge was Lock No. 2, also bridged and 700 hundred yards again to the east was a lifting road bridge leading from Jemappes to Ghlin. Lieutenant Colonel Smith placed outposts over the canal near to the bridges. Captain Rose (B Company) and Captain Innes (C Company) shared the defence of the long length of canal on the right of the railway station, close to the southern bank. Captain Tullis (D Company) held the left flank at the Pont Richebe whilst Battalion Headquarters was in the village behind the church, where the reserve company, A, was also situated. The whole of the Battalion's position was amongst a small, heavily built-up area on the edge of the coal mining district.

Swing bridge at Nimy, looking towards Mons.

As early as 6 am, just north of the bridge to Ghlin, the quietness of the morning was broken by B Company when its outpost was approached by a German cavalry patrol coming out of the mist. At 500 yards the Scots' machine gun hit the patrol, killing one and forcing the others to scatter. The fallen trooper was identified as being part of IXth Corps.

For the time being all was quiet, and soon the church bells sounded out. Many of the villagers (there was a population of about 6,000) appeared on the streets, either to go to mass or, so it seemed to the bemused soldiers, going to the station to board the holiday train that was already waiting there, to take them to their destination via Mons. They seemed quite oblivious to the imminence of fighting on their doorstep.

1/NF (Northumberland Fusiliers) were under the command of Lieutenant Colonel HS Ainslie. When they came close to the mining area near to Frameries, B and C Companies, under the Battalion's Second in Command, Major C Yatman, were detached and marched to the left and became the left flank troops of both the Brigade and the 3rd Division. They were positioned near Quaregnon, tasked with defending the lifting bridge at Mariette, a thousand yards to the left of 1/RSF. The remainder of the Battalion went into Cuesmes, some mile and a half south of Mons and a similar distance from the Condé Canal and Jemappes. Billets were found for Battalion Headquarters in the Curé's house on the village square. Just as in Jemappes, a remarkable holiday atmosphere prevailed.

Major Yatman's orders that evening had been to hold on as long as possible, so he knew that there would be no advance on the Sunday. The evening and night of the 22nd were spent in preparing

British infantry preparing to meet the invaders. For a number of years the infantry had been training to fire fifteen aimed rounds a minute – the results were devastating against a massed infantry attack.

the defence of the bridge, by A Company, and the canal bank to the right by C Company. The situation was somewhat complicated, for in reality there were two canals and therefore two bridges. The first was a short, twenty foot long bridge, that spanned the first narrow, but very deep, drainage canal and connected the south bank to the forty foot wide central tow path. Then came the lifting bridge (which lifted towards the far bank) over the sixty feet wide Condé Canal. On the north bank was the bridge keeper's house; Sergeant Panter with twelve men turned that into a small fort by loopholing the walls. The railway ran alongside the north bank, so the level crossing gates were jammed and a barbed wire barricade erected which connected the houses. A further obstacle was made on that side of the canal with some iron railings, virtually enclosing the Sergeant and his party, but leaving a small gap through which they could make their escape. The buildings on the central bank were demolished, but the ruins manned to provide support for the outpost beyond; whilst the main defence took up position in loopholed houses lining the south bank.

The men were still working on the defences when Major Yatman was summoned at about 7 am to the station in Quaregnon. There he spoke on the telephone to a man who spoke in perfect English; he was a British agent who told him that he was near the Bois de Badour, some four miles north of the canal, and that various German units were near him, which he identified. Suddenly the voice fell silent and Yatman never did discover either who the brave man was or his fate.

THE 5TH DIVISION

The first battalion of Sir Charles Fergusson's Division to arrive at the Condé Canal on the 22nd was 1/RWK (Queen's Own Royal West Kents). Lieutenant Colonel A Martyn's Battalion was to defend the three bridges at Saint Ghislain, 3,000 yards west of Quaregnon. There was a

fixed iron railway bridge on the right, not quite 2,000 yards west of the Northumberland's bridge at Mariette; a wooden one at Lock No. 3, barely a hundred yards to the left of the railway; and another lifting road bridge a thousand yards to the west of that. The Battalion's front was about 3,000 yards. D Company (Captain RGM Tulloch) would hold the railway bridge whilst C Company (Major P Hastings) was to guard the two to the left of it. These two forward companies were commanded by Major PM Buckle, the Second in Command. A and B Companies were in reserve in Hornu, two miles south.

The companies at the canal set about turning the buildings close to the canal into strong points, loopholing walls, erecting barbed wire barricades and digging trenches on the far bank. C Company had moved across because buildings on the north side obstructed their view beyond. The situation for the defenders was not helped by the ground round about consisting mainly of water meadows, useless for artillery.

Reports of the enemy by the Divisional Cyclists on the 22nd after their skirmish led to a decision to send men northwards to make contact with the enemy. At 5.30 am A Company (Captain GD Lister) received instructions to follow a cavalry patrol of 19/Hussars and the Cyclists over the canal and make a reconnaissance towards Tertre, two miles to the north; and to take up a position as far as the fork in the road on the southern edge of that village.

Shortly after 8 am the Company went over the canal and within half an hour had reached their objective. The men dug themselves in on either side of the road, about 400 yards from the village.

2/Duke of Wellington's was in support to 1/RWK and were billeted in and around the market square of Hornu. The Battalion had hardly settled in when Captain WM Ozanne, the machine-gun officer, was ordered to take his two guns forward to support 1/RWK at the railway embankment on the north side of the bridge. It was a dark night and no easy matter to drag the gun limbers over the tow path; however at 10.30 pm he met up with Captain HD Buchanan-Dunlop at Lock 3 and determined to stay with the Kents until daylight.

At 4 am on the Sunday morning some Belgian cyclists came through their position and said that they had seen large numbers of the enemy with field guns approaching the canal. The 2/Duke of Wellington's machine-gunners then went over the canal to the embankment; Captain Ozanne positioned one each side of the twenty foot high mound, the gun team on the right being commanded by Sergeant Smith. They were firmly in position by 7.30am.

The left flank battalion of 13 Brigade was 2/KOSB (King's Own Scottish Borderers), which had seven hundred reservists in its ranks. It had arrived (under the command of Lieutenant Colonel CM Stephenson) at Boussu, two miles south of the Condé Canal and two miles west of Hornu, in the afternoon of the 22nd; after a short rest it marched north to the canal, to the left of 1/RWK, and stopped at the hamlet of Les Herbieres. The Battalion's task was to hold the iron road bridge of Les Herbieres at Lock No. 4 and the thousand yards plus of canal bank that lay between there and 1/RWK. 200 yards west of the Les Herbieres road bridge was a fixed railway bridge which was the responsibility of 1/E Surreys of 14 Brigade. As in 13 Brigade sector on their right, a deep drainage canal ran alongside the main one, separated by the wide tow path and beyond it the lifting bridge. On the north bank was a short row of houses.

B and D Companies of 2/KOSB under Majors ES D'Ewes Coke and Chandos Leigh were moved up to the canal and began digging trenches. They, too, were aware that there would be no advance. General Smith-Dorrien's orders to prepare a second line of defence had dispelled that idea. Opposite the short row of houses a tall white house on the south side of the bank was turned into a machine-gun post. Lieutenant JBW Pennyman, the machine-gun officer, used the top floor to give him good observation. Houses were knocked down or fortified and barricades built. Over the bridge, some 400 yards north, the road forked to the right, the road to Tertre, a village soon to be occupied by the Germans. By dawn on the 23rd, B Company (Major Coke) was in position half a mile north of Lock No. 4 to cover the approaches. The defence of the bridge and the bank lay in the hands of D Company. To the right A (Captain LD Spencer) and C (Captain EW Macdonald) Companies had their men stretched out toward the 1/RWK position. The machine guns of the supporting battalion, 2/KOYLI (King's Own Yorkshire Light Infantry), under the command of Lieutenant Pepys, had been brought up to cover these companies.

At 7.30 am things were quiet to their front, although sounds of battle could be heard to the right. It was not until midday that things began to happen on this part of the battlefield.

As the morning progressed Major Coke and some others continued to examine buildings for their defensive potential. They found in one the occupants who had remained despite the obvious preparations for a battle. They were made most welcome and fed omelettes and given coffee to drink. One of the ladies of the house suggested that all the visitors – and there were many by now – should write their names on the tablecloth. Four years later, in November 1918, Coke, who was by then a Brigadier General (he commanded 169 Brigade of the famous 56th (London) Division from its formation in France in February 1916 to the end of the war), found himself near Les Herbieres. He went to see if he could find the house once again. It was only a ruin, but on hearing his voice two ladies came out of the cellar. In minutes they were drinking coffee and he was answering questions about the officers the ladies remembered, such as Captains Smith and Spencer and they were telling him of their experience under German occupation. In due course they produced the tablecloth, safeguarded despite the vicissitudes of the war, and presented it to Coke; it is now the cherished possession of the Regiment's Officers' Mess.

The last battalion of 13 Brigade, 2/KOYLI, with the exception of its machine guns, were in support in Boussu; they would see no action until Sunday midday when enemy shells began to fall around the brewery where they were billeted and having their lunch.

In touch with 2/KOSB on the left were 1/E Surrey of 14 Brigade. Their commanding officer, Lieutenant Colonel Longley, had brought the Battalion over from Dublin via Kingston upon Thames, where 499 reservists were added to the strength. The Battalion reached the Condé Canal on the Saturday afternoon, having made an eighteen mile approach march. It was to defend the railway bridge at Les Herbieres, which carried the major Mons to Tournai line, and a lifting road bridge, the Pont d'Hautrage, almost a mile to the left of that. South of the canal the land was a vast water meadow and to the north, on either side of a five hundred yard long railway embankment, were small woods. Nearly two thousand yards away was the large and scattered village of Hautrage. A mile south of the canal flowed the narrow River Haine. Lieutenant Colonel Longley had also been told that there would not now be an advance over the canal, and so he placed his companies accordingly. C Company (Captain JP Benson) went over the canal and deployed either side of the embankment, taking with them the machine-gun section under Lieutenant TH Darwell. On the left flank was B Company (Captain EM Woulfe-Flanagan), at the road bridge; part of the company was put over the canal to guard the fork in the road to Hautrage, a couple of hundred yards beyond the north bank, with two platoons guarding the southern end of the bridge. Between these two was D Company (Captain MJ Minogue), spread out along the south bank, and nearby was Battalion Headquarters. A Company (Captain HP Torrens) was held in reserve about 500 yards to the rear of Headquarters, in a small wood. The Battalion Second in Command (Major HS Tew) took up post to the south of the railway bridge and held responsibility for that flank. The dressing station and transport lines with the reserve ammunition were well behind Major Tew, to the left of the railway line. The East Surreys had probably the best position of all the units in the 5th Division, with good fields of fire, and Lieutenant Colonel Longley had positioned his men very effectively.

At dawn on the 23rd a patrol under Captain Campbell went forward as far as the railway station at Hautrage (blissful, happy days, before the arrival of the Belgian Dr Beeching, when every settlement seems to have had a station) and found the railwaymen busily engaged getting steam up and removing the engines and carriages south over the canal and into the British lines.

Lieutenant Colonel Longley came forward and decided that he needed better fields of fire, which could be achieved by clearing the undergrowth. He sent A Company forward to do this, and asked 2/Suffolk, the Brigade reserve, to lend him a company to help. Except for hard work in the hot and humid morning and the clank of pick and shovel, all was quiet and uneventful, at least until shortly after noon.

The left flank battalion of the whole of II Corps was 1/DCLI (Duke of Cornwall's Light Infantry). They had to guard over 3,000 yards of canal. The front extended from left of the Pont d'Hautrage to Lock No. 5, 2,000 yards away. Nearby, to the east, there was a lifting bridge which connected Thulin, two miles south of the canal, to Le Petit Crepin, five hundred yards on the north side and beyond that the large village of Pommeroeul. The frontage extended a further thousand yards to the west, but at least there were no more bridges or locks to defend along this stretch.

1/DCLI's commander, Lieutenant Colonel Martin Turner, was an extraordinary man. He was born in 1865 to middle class parents and left home at the age of 19 to enlist as a private. He was immediately bought out by his father, but left home again and this time joined the Gordon Highlanders, probably thinking that this would take him far enough away from his father this time. He served on the North West Frontier in India and was commissioned in due course into the DCLI. He went to Burma and fought in the war there and then saw service in 1897 in the Tirah campaign on the North West Frontier. He returned to Burma as Adjutant of the

Photograph taken by a British soldier at Mons. A canal boat turned into a bridge to facilitate a British withdrawal.

Burma Rifles and then returned to command the DCLI depot at Bodmin. In 1911 he took command of the 1st Battalion. He was severely wounded on the Aisne in September 1914 and ended his war as a Brigadier General, having been given command of a brigade in 1916.

Turner concentrated his Battalion along the road bridge and its approaches. The obvious line of attack would be down the long, wide and straight road from Ville Pommeroeul – the land on either side of it was water meadow.

He faced another potential problem if the enemy should breach the canal defences. Behind the canal, at its southernmost point perhaps a mile away, was the River Haine; not a particularly wide feature, but it could complicate matters if a retreat had to be made in haste, and certainly could affect the cohesion of the Battalion.

Most of the defences were put over the bridge, on the north side of the canal. B Company sent a platoon under Lieutenant Saville to take a position some four hundred yards forward on the road leading to the east side of Le Petit Crepin. He in turn sent three men, under Private Sambrook, a couple of hundred yards forward along this road. C Company took up a position over the bridge, whilst the remainder of B was concentrated at the southern bridgehead. A Company was deployed along the bank to connect with the troops to the right. D Company (Captain Woodham) were in reserve, but were spending their time preparing the defences of the bridge over the Haine, just north of Sardon. Lieutenant Colonel Turner, with his adjutant, Lieutenant AN Acland, made their advanced Headquarters in this hamlet, whilst the main Battalion Headquarters were in Thulin, several hundred yards further south – which was also the location of 5th Division Headquarters.

The two other battalions of 14 Brigade, 2/Suffolk and 2/Manchester, were deployed around Hainin, a couple of miles south of the canal; the Suffolks in support of the East Surreys and the Manchesters of the DCLI.

At 6 am on Sunday morning Private Sambrook and his two comrades were surprised to see riding slowly towards them a number of German cavalry. These men were from the 9th (Cavalry) Division, part of Marwitz's IInd (Cavalry) Corps. Von Kluck had continued to push his cavalry westwards, rather than concentrating them with his main army, as von Bülow wished. The dissipation of his cavalry force could well have had a crucial impact on the Retreat a few days later if they had been more readily available.

The cavalrymen were in no hurry, chatting as they rode, with no idea of the proximity of the British – or, indeed, the French. The three DCLI men held their fire, keeping well down in the ditch that ran alongside the road. The Germans came alongside them and one, an officer, glancing down, saw them. He fumbled for his revolver but he was too late and Private Sambrook shot him at close range. The patrol wheeled about and made off up the road, but one of the soldiers grabbed at the reins of the wounded officer's horse. He did not manage to stop it, but in all the excitement the officer's helmet fell off. In the meantime the other soldiers get up their fire, causing casualties, but the Germans got away. The three men of the outpost scrambled out of the ditch and back to Lieutenant Saville's position, carrying their helmet trophy with its bullet hole with them. It is now in the regimental museum in Bodmin.

Shortly before 7 am the Germans returned and looked for the Cornwall's outpost; not finding anyone there they continued their progress along the road towards the platoon's position. At less than a hundred yards Saville's men opened fire and once again the cavalry beat a hasty retreat, returning whence they came. Saville did not know how many he had hit, but there were a number of dead horses on the road and later in the morning villagers came in with various trophies such as swords, pistols, lances and items of uniform.

At 8 am one of the German Dragoons, badly wounded, was brought in by the villagers. He could stand, but was in abject fear, expecting to be shot. He was put on a stretcher and sent back to Battalion Headquarters. After he was examined the medical officer reported that all the man's stomach contained was oats; obviously he had been sharing the horse's rations.

The Germans had still not given up, and shortly after 8 am another cavalry patrol came up, this time along the Ville Pommeroeul road, probably oblivious of earlier events. This time the advance was taking the cavalry directly under Lieutenant Benn's machine guns, positioned at the bridge with several hundred yards of straight road along which to fire. Unfortunately, before they could be brought to bear a rifleman to the right of the bridge fired a shot, which was enough to send the cavalry back. Nevertheless, a dead horse could be seen lying in the road and shortly afterwards the wounded rider was brought in. He too was in fear of his life and begged for mercy. He was sent back to Headquarters at Thulin. The Germans were now well aware of the British left flank; but it was not until Sunday afternoon that any fighting returned to Lieutenant Colonel Turner's Battalion.

15 Brigade was put in reserve behind 13 and 14, towards the centre and west of the Condé Canal, in and around the villages of Boussu and Elouges.

The Royal Engineers had also been having a busy time. The CRE (Commander Royal Engineers) of 3rd Division was Lieutenant Colonel CS Wilson, who controlled the Division's two Field Companies, 56 and 57; the CRE of the 5th Division was Lieutenant Colonel JAS Tulloch, with his Field Companies, the 17th and 59th; they had been very industrious.

Gangs of Belgians had been recruited to assist with the construction of II Corps' second line of defence, and these needed to be supervised. However, the first priority

Defending the rail bridge.

was the bridges and their preparation for demolition.

The sappers faced a real problem. There was a severe shortage of explosives – but more acute was the insufficient number of fuses. A short time before mobilisation the fuze instantaneous had been withdrawn (due to store changing). The speed of mobilisation meant that they had not been replaced. They would have to rely upon safety fuse and electrical firing, and these exploders were only issued on the basis of one per section. It would mean that to explode more than one charge simultaneously would require each length of fuse to be of the same length and all to be fired at the same time. As the iron girder bridges required multiple charges, much ingenuity would be required. There were eighteen bridges in total, more than there were officers to take charge, so much of the work fell upon junior NCOs.

At 2.30 am on the 23rd the sappers of the 3rd Division were told to prepare the bridges in their area for demolition but were further instructed at 8.53 am that nothing must be destroyed until the Division's retirement became necessary. The engineers of the 5th Division were busily engaged in preparing houses to be used as strong points; though the bridges had been reconnoitred, nothing as yet had been done about preparing them for destruction.

It took some time to get the men of the 56th and 57th on to the bridges, broadcast as they were on the task of preparing the second line. Nothing could be done until 6.30 am; Major NJ Hopkins of the 56th Fd Coy sent men into Mons in search of more explosives, but they returned empty handed. By 8 am the task had begun, but in the curve of the canal from the top near Nimy and down to Obourg firing had already commenced, so that it was impossible to work on these bridges.

8AM – MIDDAY:

BATTLES OF THE MONS SALIENT BEGINS

At about 8.30 am the attack by the 85th and 86th Fusiliers under the protection of a heavy bombardment began against the Middlesex on the right of the salient's tip at Mons. They were firing from across the canal and some of them got into houses on the hillside of Obourg and put strong pressure on D Company in the station. It was in this initial attack that Private Parr was killed.

On the left of the Battalion, opposite B Company, machine-gunners saw a German battery unlimbering their guns almost a mile away across the flat land below the hill; these were put under heavy fire and the gunners departed to seek an alternative site.

Gradually the German infantry attack spread further around the bend towards the bridge at Rue des Bragnons. At about this time, Major Hopkins was ready to send his engineers to demolish the bridges on 4/Middx front; two platoons of C Company of 2/RIrR (Royal Irish Regiment) went with the section to the bridge over the Canal du Centre at Obourg. However, when Captain Fitzgerald arrived it was already too late, the enemy were positioned on the far side of the bridge, making it impossible for the sappers to operate. The engineers also tried to get to the Rue des Bragnons bridge, but again the Germans had arrived first. The commander of the RE section, Lieutenant HW Holt, was killed when the Germans rushed his section; he has the dubious distinction of being the first Royal Engineer officer killed in the War. Sergeant Miles and the rest of the section were captured. Thus, all the bridges in front of 4/Middx were intact and available to the enemy.

The German infantry began to come towards the canal at about 10 am, advancing in solid blocks with rifles at the trail, firing from the hip. The intention was to storm by sheer impact of numbers. The rifle and machine-gun fire of 4/Middx tore great gaps in the compact ranks; but still they came on and, despite their awful losses, the sheer number of them forced the bridges and by 10.30 am they were over the canal.

At the railway station almost all of the defenders had been either killed or wounded, including the detachment's commander, Lieutenant ABW Allistone, wounded and captured. An unknown last man at the barricade on the station roof remained at his post; although wounded, he could still fire his rifle. By his actions he helped those who were physically able to make good their escape; in due course this nameless hero was killed.

Captain Glass was wounded by the time his D Company withdrew to the convent; whilst Major Davy was killed by the time that B Company was forced back to the railway cutting. At 11 am 4/Middx's line had not been broken, but it had been squeezed back so that it was well south of the canal and surrounding the group of buildings in front of the communal cemetery, including the convent and the hospital. Lieutenant Colonel Hull called on 2/RIrR (commanded by Lieutenant Colonel St. J Cox) to come up in support, which was done promptly.

4/RF stood to at daybreak after a gruelling night of digging and preparing their defences. They had heard the Germans moving about in the large wood on the far side of the canal. Shortly before 8 am a cavalry patrol was seen coming towards the opposite bank of the road bridge, which had been swung back. Galloping straight towards it, unaware of the proximity of the Fusiliers, the officer and six men were brought to an abrupt halt when the Londoners opened fire, killing four of them and wounding the officer, knocking him off his horse. The remaining two members of the patrol escaped, fleeing back into the wood. Quickly men dashed across the bridge and brought the officer in; he turned out to be Lieutenant von Arnim, the son of Sixt von Arnim, commander of IVth Corps, whose troops would soon be engaged against 14 Brigade. The Lieutenant was a member of the 'Death's Head' Hussars, and his notebook showed that he had been observing the British positions from the wood, yet had no idea of the scale of the force on the opposite side of the canal.

The Germans began their attack against 4/RF at about 10 am, led by the 84th Regiment in solid blocks, who advanced under a barrage of artillery fire. At a thousand yards the targets could not be missed and their leading sections of four abreast were destroyed, causing the whole regiment to retire back to the wood. After a heavy bombardment on the Fusiliers' trenches they came on again; the Royal Artillery could not reach them from the awkward firing positions that they had been able to find. Casualties began to mount, particularly amongst the officers. Lieutenant Mead was sent up from Nimy railway station to assist but was almost immediately wounded in the head. He returned to have it dressed and then went back without hesitation, whistling as he went, to be shot again through the head, this time fatally. By this time Captain Ashburner was wounded and Captain Fred Forster had been killed.

The Germans were still being held at bay, the two machine guns on the railway bridge in particular doing great execution, though suffering losses amongst their crews as well. By 11 am the machine-gun officer, Lieutenant Maurice Dease, had been wounded twice. Each time one of the guns stopped firing he went forward from his trench on the embankment some fifty yards back to find out why; and then returned once more with replacements or more ammunition.

C Company remained under constant bombardment; the road bridge was impassable because it had been swung back, but the valiant Germans still came forward to try and force a crossing over the railway bridge. Casualties amongst C Company continued to mount despite reinforcements; Captain Bowden Smith died of wounds and Lieutenant EC Smith was killed outright.

Major Howard had not given up all hope of destroying the railway and road bridges at Nimy. He sent one of his section commanders, Lieutenant AF Day to deal with them; but Day found that he had not got enough explosive to do both. In any case, the enemy fire was devastating and he could not get into suitable positions to lay charges. Nevertheless, he remained close to the railway bridge to await his opportunity. Further to the left things were altogether quieter, even though the men of 4/RF here did come under sporadic rifle and shell fire from across the canal. They had sunk the barges and other craft; and now they simply awaited their turn to be attacked. Corporal A Payne (later to become a Major) of 57 Fd Coy, with his six sappers, had laid his charges carefully at the road bridge to Ghlin and the nearby railway bridge. He did not have an electric exploder and so would have to set the charges off simultaneously with equal lengths of safety fuse. He waited the word of command to destroy the bridges.

Over to the left, before Jemappes, at the start of the Condé Canal, 1/RSF could hear the battle raging to their right but before them all was relatively quiet. At 10.30 am the artillery of IIIrd Corps opened fire on them, soon to be followed by the densely packed columns of infantry belonging to the 6th Division coming across the water meadows from the wood behind Ghlin. After being received with the accurate and rapid fire of the Scots, they spread out and came forward in rushes in small units. Some company commander had had the sense to abandon the suicidal formation used in most places that morning.

Lieutenant Colonel Smith had already withdrawn his posts north of the canal, and his Battalion's concentrated fire stopped the enemy not more than 200 yards from the Pont Richebe, in the built-up area to the left of the railway station. They would succeed in holding the 6th Division until early in the afternoon.

The sappers of 57 Fd Coy were here as well; Lieutenant PK Boulnois had left Corporal Jarvis and

Sapper Neary to deal with the bridge over Lock No. 2, 800 yards east of Pont Richebe, when it was time so to do. Boulnois had with him four NCOs and four sappers on bicycles, with a forage cart loaded with explosives and a drum of cable. His responsibilities were the bridges from the right of Jemappes station to the lifting bridge at Mariette, the latter defended by 1/NF on 9 Brigade's left flank. The party was divided into pairs, one to each bridge; leaving explosives and cable at each, he arranged that he would return with his exploder and blow each in turn. Because the Mariette Bridge promised to be the most difficult, that was entrusted to his senior NCO, Sergeant Smith, and Sapper Dabell. The senior engineer officer at 9 Brigade's bridges was Captain Theodore Wright, the adjutant to 3 Division's CRE. He had a car and a roving commission from Mariette to the two bridges at Nimy. The morning for all these sappers was busy and dangerous, though they were constricted by the requirement to await orders before they could blow their bridges. Nevertheless, all the barges and boats, some of them homes, were sunk, to the misery of some of the owners who could only stand and watch it happening.

At midday, all the bridges in the 3rd and 5th divisional areas were still intact.

By 9 am Sergeant Panter, 1/NF, had seen nothing from his strongpoint in the bridge keeper's cottage north of the canal. Sergeant Johnson was with a small party in a coal shed on the central bank, equally alert. C Company were busy improving their trenches on either side of the road crossing the south bank of the canal; whilst B Company was engaged in similar activity at the road junction a hundred yards further south. Major Yatman put his detachment's Headquarters 300 yards further

Much of the fighting at Mons took place in built up areas from which much of the civilian population had not had time to flee.

down the road at the railway station. At mid-morning the sound of gunfire could be heard to the right; whilst two miles to the west, where 1/RWK held the canal at Saint Ghislain, a large battle was obviously taking place. Not a shell had fallen on Mariette before 10.30 am, almost as though the Germans had forgotten about the bridge here and were concentrating on those to the left and at Jemappes.

Sergeant Panter suddenly saw a column of German infantry entering the main street in front of them, four abreast, and proceeding as if unaware of the British presence. Within minutes the fire of him and his men had scattered the enemy, leaving many dead and wounded lying in the street. At 11 am Panter withdrew his small garrison back over the canal into C Company's trenches; as he did so the enemy artillery began to shell the northern bank where he had been. The fire lifted and the bombardment passed over the canal and also onto the central bank between the two canals, killing Sergeant Johnson. The three men who were with him were unable to make their escape due to the crossfire across the bridge. They took shelter in the cellar, where they remained until the battle had passed over them completely. They then emerged and managed to catch up with their battalion five days later when it had marched many miles to the south.

1/Lincoln, the fourth battalion in 9/Brigade, was in reserve in Cuesmes, a mile and a half south west of Mons; on Sunday morning they were prepared to move to whatever part of the battlefield needed their assistance. At midday they were called upon to block the roads from the town at the south west corner, erecting four barricades. Whilst engaged in this they were not aware of how grateful 4/RF would be for their assistance an hour or so later.

1/RWK (13 Brigade) found themselves engaged in fighting soon after 8 am. They had entrenched themselves and covered the three bridges in their sector. Did they but know it, they were only three miles from the concentration area of the German 5th Division. To the north of the canal was A Company, not far from Tertre, covering the approaches from Badour and waiting for the enemy which Cyclists had reported seeing in large numbers in and beyond the village. Meanwhile four 18 pdrs of 120 Battery had been brought forward to just south of the canal. At 8.15 am four of the Divisional Cyclists came down the road from Tertre at full speed and flung themselves down into the ditch where Lieutenant Gore's men were digging in. [Gore himself would be killed at Neuve Chapelle two months later.] They reported that the rest of the detachment had been blown to pieces by the enemy's artillery. Within minutes of this some hundreds of infantry began to come towards the Kents from the open land between the village and railway embankment on the right. As everywhere else, this was the first time 1/RWK had seen solid ranks of infantry steadily marching towards them;

Massed German infantry attack.

'...in our first battle we had been badly beaten, and by the English – by the English we had so laughed at a few hours before.'

Captain Lister's men could not miss. These Germans were from 3 Battalion, 12th Brandenburg Grenadiers; their brave advance was brought to a halt with fearful casualties. The Germans then brought a battery of artillery into action and another body of infantry began to advance; in the meantime more of them, 1 Battalion, began to advance out of Tertre down the left hand side of the road through the wooded area.

(For an outstanding account of this battle from the German perspective, you should make every endeavour to get hold of a copy of The Advance from Mons by Captain Walter Bloem, who commanded B Company, 1 Battalion, 12th Brandenburg Grenadiers in the battle. It is a quite remarkable book; Bloem comments on this day's fighting:

'A bad defeat, there could be no gainsaying it; in our first battle we had been badly beaten, and by the English – by the English we had so laughed at a few hours before.'

What is even more remarkable about this book is that it was published in Germany, by this well-established novelist, in 1916.)

Over on the railway embankment Captain Ozanne, commanding the two 2/Duke of Wellington's machine guns, had come across his first German. At 10 am, before he went into action against the Brandenburger's assaulting 1/RWK to his left, he had gone 200 yards in front of his emplacements and found a track that ran underneath the embankment; where he came face to face with a German cavalryman. Equally shocked, the German bolted off on his horse and Ozanne raced back the way he had come, neither having the presence of mind to draw a weapon. On returning to his guns he opened fire on more of the cavalry that had emerged from the wood, 500 yards to his left. Later in the day he would be wounded and have a remarkable escape from capture when, at 11 pm, he found a train about to leave a siding from Saint Ghislain station, arriving in Amiens some hours later.

A Company had now become so depleted that it was unable to withstand the pressure from the overwhelming number of Brandenburgers; shortly before noon the men retired, Major Beresford then brought B Company over to replace them, whilst the field guns got right up to the canal to support them. A Company had lost severely in the morning's fighting: one officer dead, two wounded and 93 other ranks killed, wounded or missing. During the withdrawal of A Company, Private Donovan of C Company saw Lieutenant Bell struggling to bring in a wounded man of A Company. He went forward to help, regardless of the lead mayhem around him; in due course he received the DCM for this action, the first won by the Battalion in the War.

'He went forward to help, regardless of the lead mayhem around him; in due course he received the DCM for this action, the first won by the Battalion in the War.'

The battle at Saint Ghislain continued throughout the afternoon, only ending at nightfall.

2/KOSB could only sit tight and listen – the men of von Kluck's army, his human scythe, did not reach their position until shortly after midday. 2/KOYLI were in the rear, but their lunchtime at the brewery in Boussu was to be rudely disturbed by enemy artillery. It was to be the last hot meal, disrupted or not, that the Battalion was to enjoy for some days to come. One man was hit and the rest bolted their food down. Lieutenant Pepys hurriedly returned to his machine-guns at the canal embankment; the rest of the Battalion would not see action (apart from being shelled) until 2.30 pm. 1/East Surrey also spent a quiet morning – nothing at all happened on their front; they could only listen and wonder as to what was taking place on their right. 1/DCLI also had a quiet morning, after the initial early morning flurry of excitement with Private Sambrook and German cavalry.

15 Brigade's four battalions were employed in digging defences two and three miles south of the canal, at Wasmes, Elouges and Paturages. Shells had not fallen far from them, but they would not see the real war until the following day.

MONS: AFTERNOON 23RD AUGUST

8 BRIGADE AND 4TH ROYAL FUSILIERS

The German infantry were now pouring across the Canal du Centre bridges in the Middlesex sector and were working their way round the right flank of D Company, moving out of Havre Wood, threatening to encircle the Company. On the northern, left, flank the Germans had reached the railway cutting where Major Davy, commanding B Company, had already been killed. Major Abell, taking A Company towards it, hoping to prevent the Battalion from being encircled, was also killed. The machine-gun officer, Lieutenant Sloane-Stanley, was wounded, but still there in the centre of the two front line companies, north east of the cemetery, with his surviving gun. In front of him he calculated that six enemy guns were in action. With six volunteers he intended to stay until overrun and captured. The German artillery had brought up more guns to the slopes on the far side of the canal and the whole of the sector east of Mons was being saturated with shell fire.

2/RIrR received the call for help from Lieutenant Colonel Hull whilst they were in the midst of their lunch, the last prepared one they would have for some time. They had heard the battle drawing closer and had been under shell fire since the middle of the morning. Lieutenant Colonel Cox sent A Company and two platoons from each of B and C, under the command of Major St Leger, at the double to the quarry above the cemetery. D Company under Captain Elliott moved to the cemetery, where C Company of 4/Middx were hanging on to their position. Two sections from A Company of 2/RIrR were put in the hollow at the western exit of the cemetery and at the major crossroads 200 yards beyond. Lieutenant FL Rushton, the Transport Officer, took the Irish machine guns well forward, close to the remaining one of 4/Middx, between A and C Companies.

The battlefield of 4/Middx gradually became that of 2/RIrR. Already the commander of A Company, Captain Mellor, had been killed by a shell burst as he went forward with Major St Leger. The whole Battalion, by 2 pm, was involved in an arc covering the crossroads at the Faubourg Barthelemy and the road to Binches and Harmignies. To the rear was the large Bois la Haut, the trees covering the hill which rose some five hundred feet high.

The battered remnants of 4/Middx who had survived the enemy onslaught thus far attempted to withdraw from in front of the cemetery. The Mental Hospital in front and to the right of the cemetery had caught fire, and hundreds of terrified inmates fled across the fields into the British defence lines, adding a macabre dimension to the confusion. Numbers were killed, whilst behind them came the advancing Germans, only a few hundred yards away and now dominating the battlefield;

they were managing to infiltrate the Irish and Middlesex positions through the confusion of streets surrounding the cemetery. Captain Oliver withdrew with the remnants of C Company after the Middlesex machine gun was finally silenced and made for the large building which was the convent, a few hundred yards to the north of the cemetery. He wanted to get his horse out of the stables, but found that the Germans were already there. He took his men to the high wall at the back, but the gate was locked; one of his men blew it off, but injured himself in the process. Emerging from the gate on the Nimy Road, he and his men ran into crossfire; some fell, but the survivors crossed the road and went into the hollow where they found Lieutenant Ferguson with some men of the Irish A Company.

By 3.30 pm Lieutenant Colonel Hull's survivors had left the battlefield, though there remained some who were unable to move back with the rest and who were eventually overrun as they became isolated. Unfortunately the trials were not over for 4/Middx. They took the narrow road behind the west side of the hill and marched towards the tiny village of Hyon; the Germans were already there. They had managed to work their way from Nimy between the Middlesex and 4/RF. Here the Middlesex fought their last battle of the day and another sixty men became casualties. Eventually they reached Nouvelles, a few miles further south, and the roll call on that summer's evening showed that they only numbered 275. Fifteen officers were casualties, of whom five were killed and ten wounded and taken prisoner (including the Battalion Medical Officer, Captain Terry, who was himself wounded but opted to remain behind to look after the casualties). 453 other ranks were casualties, of whom ninety were killed; but a hundred of these reappeared over the next days as II Corps proceeded with the retreat. Still, given that the

> 'At Nimy, Dease realised that both his guns had ceased firing; he went forward once more and was hit for the third time, mortally wounded.'

total British casualty count for the Battle of Mons was some 1,600, this was a very significant proportion of the total, well over 20 per cent.

By 1 pm the situation of Lieutenant Colonel McMahon's 4/RF was desperate. Although the railway bridge had still not been forced, C (also known as Y) Company had almost eighty casualties. Lieutenant Dease, twice wounded, had lost almost all of his machine-gun section and the left hand gun had been knocked out.

Round the corner at Lock No. 6 and the two bridges, the railway running under the Ghlin road bridge, Captain Byng and D (Z) Company had been under fire and direct frontal attack from the woods (about a mile away) and the open land in front for some hours. The defenders' fire had kept the (initially) massed ranks of Germans at bay, but by 1 pm the Germans had learnt their lesson and Byng had moved his men back to the canal. Corporal Payne of 57 Fd Coy had everything prepared to demolish the bridges as soon as the Fusiliers got across. The enemy artillery fire fell on the men of D Company as they ran back over the bridge, covered by Major Mallock's rearguard from A (W) Company. As the last man stumbled across, Corporal Payne and his men lit the six lengths of safety fuse and ran across the railway lines under the bridge. Because of the noise of bursting shells and the general sound of battle, Payne could not hear if his charges had exploded, but some evidently had as large pieces of the bridge came hurtling down behind him as he ran.

At 1.10 pm the Battalion received its first order to retire.

At Nimy, Dease realised that both his guns had ceased firing; he went forward once more and was hit for the third time, mortally wounded. There was no one left alive at the guns, and only one in the machine-gun section.

Railway bridge at Nimy where Lieutenant Dease and Private Godley won their Victoria Crosses. This is not the original bridge – it was destroyed twice in the Second World War – however, the dimensions of the present-day bridge are the same as the original 1914 one.

49

The position of Private Godley's machine gun on the bridge.

Only the right hand gun was fit to use, and that had bullet holes in its water jacket. Lieutenant Steele asked for volunteers who could use the gun, and Private Sidney Frank Godley of the machine-gun section, already wounded, said that he could. Moving forward he cleared out the position and set to work firing across the water into the enemy infantry. Lieutenant Day of 57 Fd Coy had remained close by the bridge in the hope of getting a chance to fix demolition charges, but the opportunity never came and during the morning he was wounded and, in due course, captured. With the sole machine gun still firing, Lieutenant Steele carried Dease back to the rear, where he died.

At 1.40 pm McMahon received the order to retire; with Godley remaining at his gun the

> 'Lieutenant Steele asked for volunteers who could use the gun, and Private Sidney Frank Godley of the machine-gun section, already wounded, said that he could.'

survivors of the 4th Royal Fusiliers withdrew back into Mons.

A brave German, Musketier Oscar Niemeyer, went into the canal, swam over to the road bridge and operated the machinery to swing it back into position over the canal. He was shot and killed by the British in the process. But nothing could now stop the hordes of German infantry from pouring over the canal, especially as Godley had been wounded again and his gun had become too damaged to fire.

They harassed the Fusiliers as they fell back and set fire to the housing; they also herded a large number of civilians in front of them. This forced a number of Fusiliers, who were manning a barricade across the main street, to fall back into Mons, as they could not fire into that crowd. The four guns of 107 Battery also withdrew from Mons. The first battalion of Brigadier General Shaw's 9 Brigade to withdraw from Mons fell back through the winding and narrow streets towards the small village of Ciply, two miles away. Their retreat was covered by 1/Lincoln, who were dug in at the southern exits of Mons.

4/RF suffered more than 150 casualties. In the course of their fighting at Mons they had the honour to win the first two of the war, VCs, Dease and Godley. Maurice Dease's was gazetted first. Godley heard about his VC when he was recovering from his severe wounds as a prisoner; the news was given to him by the Commandant of the PoW camp.

At 10 am on 24 August 4th Royal Fusiliers withdrew from the Mons salient.

Now that all the bridges from Nimy to Obourg were available to the enemy, and with two battalions out of the fight, the full force of the enemy fell on 2/RIrR and

Private Sidney Frank Godley VC.

1/Gordons (Gordon Highlanders), commanded by Lieutenant Colonel FH Neish. In front of their curved perimeter line of only 800 yards radius from the major road junction at the Faubourg Barthelmy were the 85th (Bremen) and 35th Infantry Regiments; coming down through Mons, after 4/RF's withdrawal, was the 84th (Schleswig) Regiment. The Gordons had entrenched themselves along the main road to Harmignies in a position running south easterly from the road junction and on the forward slope of the hilly Bois la Haut. Their Headquarters were on the western slope in a large house. The whole area was thickly wooded. On top of the hill and at both ends were the three batteries of artillery from XL Field Brigade RA, the 6th, 23rd and 49th. A mile below the Gordons, and along the same road, was Lieutenant Colonel McMicking's 2/RS (Royal Scots). There were still three battalions of 8 Brigade to fend off the German attack on the Mons Salient.

Since 1.30pm, when the Middlesex had begun to withdraw, the machine guns of 2/RIrR had been out of action. Sergeant J Whittington recovered one and brought it back to the crossroads and got it into action. D Company, after their first advance to the quarry, had been so badly mauled that it was withdrawn back to Hyon, behind the hill, neither the Germans or the Middlesex having yet got there. When Quarter Master Sergeant Fitzpatrick saw this happening he collected about forty men from the Transport Lines – drivers, cooks, orderlies – and placed himself under the orders of Major Simpson. This officer commanded a company of Gordons at the crossroads and Fitzpatrick's men were put into a trench on the right hand side of the road, looking down the slope towards the right hand side of the mental hospital. Despite all that happened later in the day he remained in the position until 11 pm. When the position was invested by the enemy he scattered them with rapid fire and withdrew with eighteen survivors of his party. He was awarded the DCM.

Major St Leger brought his men back to the left hand fork of the crossroads in front of Gendebien Chateau. This building was being used by the medical officer (Major Long) as a first aid post; Red Cross flags hung from the windows and one was placed on the roof. Notwithstanding this it was hit by shells in the early afternoon and set on fire. All the casualties were evacuated into the surrounding woods, though the wounded commander of 49th Battery, Major JS Maidlow, and Private CH Jackson died in the ruins. Major Lyon, 6 Battery, was hit whilst galloping along the road towards his battery on the hill, and fell from his horse. Private Redmond of the Royal Irish and two gallant Gordons leapt out of their trench near to the crossroads, despite the shelling and heavy firing, and carried him to the makeshift hospital; he survived the subsequent fire.

'When the position was invested by the enemy he scattered them with rapid fire and withdrew with eighteen survivors of his party.'

A Company had by now lost all of its officers; Major St Leger, gathering all the men that he could, put them on the edge of the road looking down the slope of the ridge and across the shallow valley towards the cemetery a thousand yards away, and through which hundreds of Germans were pouring. Major Panter-Downes (commanding C Company) arrived and was directed to hold the position. The leading ranks of the enemy began swarming up the slope, firing from the hip as they came. Panter-Downes ordered his men (only about thirty of them) to fix bayonets and with Lieutenant Shine, who had previously been down in the valley, they charged at the Germans, who were now less than fifty yards away, and routed them. This had a cost, there were thirty or so casualties, including Shine, who was mortally wounded.

200 yards to the right Fitzpatrick's party, with the aid of the machine gun rescued by Sergeant Whittington on the right, was causing havoc in the valley. At about this time the Battalion's adjutant, Lieutenant REG Phillips, was severely wounded. Impossible to move him because of the extent of his injuries, he was taken prisoner in the evening.

There were some buildings on the eastern side of the road junction where some of the men had taken cover, firing from holes in the walls. At the road junction were two of the guns of 23 Battery, but the bombardment forced their withdrawal up the hill.

By the middle of the afternoon the Battalion had become scattered and depleted, so it was necessary to leave the crossroad position and retire behind the hill. Fitzpatrick remained, as did the Gordons, whose turn it now was to stop the Germans, helped considerably by the fire from 23 Battery on the hill; the advance of the enemy suddenly provided excellent targets. Between them the enemy was halted some 300 yards from the foot of the hill.

The land at the western side of the hill is flat and marshy, with a thin stream running through it. The Irish re-formed here; Lieutenant AMS Tandy and the survivors of A Company lined the road along each side of the narrow bridge and looked north towards Mons, as the last of 4/Middx came through en route for Hyon. B Company of the Irish had also come down the narrow road behind the hill and proceeded to climb up the very steep wooded slope in a fruitless search for the Gordons, who were mistakenly thought to be at the top. B Company returned down the hill, exhausted.

In Hyon it was becoming clear to Brigadier General Doran that he would have to move his Headquarters back. On the other hand he wanted to ensure that his Brigade was relatively safe, and he was desperate to make contact with the Gordons. Sometime before 5 pm he came up to 2/RIrR and led B and C Companies back up the narrow, cobbled lane at the foot of the hill. They could hear the battle going on to the left as the withdrawing 4/Middx ran into the Germans coming down from Mons. Within a couple of hundred yards of setting off along the lane they saw the Germans ahead of them. There was no room for manoeuvre, so the Irish had to return to the bottom of the hill and to the open land between it and the main road.

At 6 pm the Gordons were still holding their line on the main road, defying the enemy who seemed to have reverted to their tactics of pressing forward in massed, closed ranks. But the pressure was telling. The 18 pdrs on top of the hill had to be rescued; a platoon of Gordons under the command of Lieutenant IBN Hamilton was sent to extricate them, but these men did not realise that Hyon was in German hands.

The only way to extract the guns was down the back of the hill and along the narrow road, but as they moved along the lane they ran into a road block where a similar narrow lane crossed the bridge from Hyon to join the lane they were using. The leading horses were killed and the guns fell off the road into a ditch on the right. Nothing daunted, one group of Gordons chased off the Germans at the point of the bayonet, whilst another helped the gunners drag the horses and guns back up onto the road and then got away to join the Irish further along.

To the right of the Gordons were 2/RS (Royal Scots). They had been in position all day some two miles down from the crossroads, spread out along the main road. Facing them was open and flat land, looking eastwards towards St Symphorien and Villers Ghislain. On their right were 1/IG (Irish Guards), of 4 (Guards) Brigade, 2nd Division, part of Haig's Ist Corps. They had an excellent field of fire, but except for the occasional shot at German cyclists, they had had a very quiet morning, in stark contrast to the raging sounds of battle coming from their left. Late in the afternoon, as the enemy attacked the Gordons to the north, a long line of German infantry came towards the forward companies, A and D, under the command of Major Tweedie. They were assisted in the defence by the Battalion machine guns under Lieutenant Laidley. The storm of defensive fire destroyed the German attack, bringing it to a halt 300 yards from the road in the flat and treeless fields. These soldiers from Bremen would wait until dusk before their next attempt.

With dark the Gordons withdrew, as did Fitzpatrick and his remnant; Major St Leger entrenched the survivors of the Irish along the track running from the bottom south east corner of the hill to the main road from Harmignies to Mons. This position was adopted to protect the guns of XL Field Brigade that were now gathered there, having escaped from their positions at Bois la Haut; and to stem any further German advances.

At 8 pm the Germans attacked the two Scottish battalions again, both from across the main road and from the flattish slopes coming down from the eastern edge of the hill. The attack from this latter point, especially as it was almost dark, was so sudden that four

'The leading horses were killed and the guns fell off the road into a ditch on the right.'

of the guns were temporarily lost, though a bayonet charge recovered them.

Shortly after this scrap the defenders could hear bugle calls. They were German, calling a halt to the fighting of the day. German losses had been tremendous; one estimate put them at more than 6,000 in Mons alone. The 75th (Bremen) regiment had lost six officers and 376 other ranks in one attack.

At 10 pm the British finally withdrew from these positions, bringing the guns with them, none of which had been lost during the day. The column passed on unhindered by the Germans and arrived at Nouvelles at 4.30 am on Monday 24 August. The Royal Irish had suffered 225 casualties, including five officers killed and five wounded. The Gordons (with 24 casualties) and the Royal Scots had got off very lightly. However, the battles in this part of Mons, involving five battalions and 1/Lincoln on the western fringes, had cost IInd Corps a thousand men. This was not a large number – indeed by comparison with later figures (even on 24 August) lost at Le Cateau, the Aisne and First Ypres, not to mention the vast battles later on in 1915 at Loos and the cataclysms on the Somme and in the Salient and the Hindenburg Line it is small – but the battle had been enormously significant for the well-being of the allied cause.

MONS: THE AFTERNOON FROM SAINT GHISLAIN TO LES HERBIERES AND THE ACTION OF 13 BRIGADE.

To the immediate right of 1/RWK were the 2/Duke of Wellington's. Captain Ozanne with his machine guns at the railway embankment had helped Lieutenant Colonel Martyn's men halt the attack of 12/Brandenburg; and for their efforts spent most of their time under shellfire. They could see the Germans sheltering behind corn stooks in the fields and fired on them intermittently; at 3 pm a shell burst in front of his emplacement, shattering his arm and wounding others.

He was able to make his way, along with the other wounded, back to the railway bridge and sheltered under it until nightfall. The bridge had already been prepared for demolition and nearby was Corporal Marsden of 17 Fd Coy ready to do the task. Whilst Ozanne was taking shelter there the Germans shelled the railway line and its bridge heavily, blowing off some of the gun cotton charges. The Corporal, despite the heavy bombardment, replaced them and the connecting leads. His work done, he returned to the south side, waiting for the exploder to arrive. Later on, whilst watching the action through a telescope, he was hit by shell fire and killed.

Lieutenant O'Kelly took a platoon of fifty-four men up to the canal on the right of the embankment at 1.30 pm. He came under fire from the direction of Mariette, where shortly the Northumberlands were to begin their retirement. Apart from some shelling, which generally went over their heads, these men came to no harm, but at 3pm O'Kelly saw a mass of infantry coming towards him across the open fields. Opening fire into the closed ranks, the enemy suffered fearful casualties, but 'as fast as they fell others came to take their place; each of my men must have fired hundreds of rounds'.

By 5pm they had come within 300 yards of O'Kelly's platoon and he ordered his men to fix bayonets. But then the Germans stopped and shortly afterwards the men heard the sound of bugles and the attackers started to melt away – for the moment at least, they had had enough. At 6pm he was ordered to retire, having suffered three killed and twelve wounded.

Captain RC Carter had taken B Company over the canal at about the same time as O'Kelly had gone forward. He put the men into buildings to the right of the road bridge near Lock No. 3. The Brandenburgers had slowed down since their battle with the Kents and Carter's orders were to fire at only good targets and not to give their position away in order to avoid artillery retaliation. Lieutenant-Colonel Gibbs had come up to examine the positions in the front line close to the canal; his orderly, Private Shellabear, was killed just a few yards from him at 3pm. At 4.30pm Brigadier-General Cuthbert sent an order to strengthen the right flank of his 13 Brigade, Major EN Townsend took A Company towards Mariette and told Captain FV Jenkins to stay with D Company in reserve on the square at St Ghislain. 2/Duke of Wellington's stayed where they were, the Brandenburgers having given up their attack for the day; the Battalion had only suffered three casualties amongst the officers thus far, all wounded.

1/RWK and 2/Duke of Wellington's were responsible for four other bridges in 13 Brigade's sector. There was a lifting bridge at Lock No. 3, 200 yards to the left of the railway where Corporal Marsden was killed; a large lifting bridge carrying the main road from St Ghislain to Tertre, in the centre of 1/RWK's sector and where B Company of 2/Duke of Wellington's held the sheds on the north bank; only six feet to its left was a wooden bridge; and there was a lifting bridge 500 yards further on. Lieutenant Godsell was responsible for all of these bridges.

At 2pm Brigadier-General Cuthbert sent for him and said that he wanted them all demolished. The road bridge was a problem because it was constantly in use carrying orderlies, ammunition, wounded men and everything required by the infantry on the north side. The adjacent foot bridge could not deal with this sort of traffic, whilst to complicate matters it would be necessary to raise the road bridge in order to fix the charges.

Godsell made Corporal Gerachty and two men responsible for the Lock bridge; whilst Corporal Taylor was sent to the bridge west of the main one. Because of the heavy firing none of the bridges could be blown in

> 'Opening fire into the closed ranks, the enemy suffered fearful casualties, but "as fast as they fell others came to take their place; each of my men must have fired hundreds of rounds."'

the afternoon; in any case there was only one exploder and that would be used, as a priority, at the railway bridge. The road bridge and its small neighbour had to be blown at the same time, for fear of creating a mutual explosion; and they could not be destroyed until the men on the far bank had been withdrawn. Lieutenant Godsell had to wait.

2/KOSB had been waiting for their turn to get involved in the fighting all morning; they were not to be kept waiting overlong as the German IIIrd and IVth Corps moved around to swing against Smith-Dorrien's flank. Major AE Haig, the Second in Command, had his observation post alongside Lieutenant Pennyman's machine-guns at the top of the white house. At 1pm he saw Germans moving diagonally across his front. They were coming in a south westerly direction from Tertre, heading for the bridge; they were a party of Brandenburg Grenadiers, led by an officer who stood out because of his bandaged head. Haig could see that they were being cautious, but they also seemed to be unaware that there was anybody in front of them. They advanced in small groups over the water meadows, cutting the barbed wire fences as they came, Haig quickly informed Major Chandos Leigh's B Company on the far side of the canal as to what was happening; they brought the advance to a halt by their rifle fire. Haig reinforced their position, whilst the Germans commenced to bring their artillery to bear.

In the course of the bombardment the lock house and the cottage, whose occupants had welcomed the Borderers earlier, were hit; Haig saw the people, carrying a canary (strange what the memory recalls) disappear into the Battalion's lines.

Haig reinforced D Company with some of A Company; D Company moved forward to get clear of the houses now under heavy shellfire. This, unintentionally, became a counter-attack, and men began to fall as the Grenadiers opened up with machine-guns and the artillery showered them with shrapnel. In addition, the machine-guns in the white house which had been searching the woodlands from which the Germans had emerged with their fire, came under artillery fire; Pennyman was forced to take them out to a less obvious position.

At 3pm Major Haig ordered a retirement from the advanced positions to the canal; Major Leigh, who had won the DSO in South Africa, and had been wounded somewhere in the water meadows, could not be found and had to be left behind. He died shortly afterwards in German captivity. Other casualties included the Medical Officer, Captain Gibbon, and Captain Kennedy, both wounded; CSM Wilson was mortally wounded and Sergeants Adair and Murray were wounded – the latter would be killed on the Somme. Corporal Field was shot through the forehead but made a miraculous recovery in a German hospital; in all the Battalion suffered about a hundred casualties.

Lieutenant Pottinger of 1/ Fd Coy had been waiting at No. 4 Lock bridge since the early afternoon, waiting for the infantry to retire and for permission from Lieutenant-Colonel Stephenson to blow it. This was not forthcoming until later in the evening and when the Germans were almost on the bridge. To Pottinger's dismay the charges would not go off; resourcefully, and using his skill as one of the army's best shots, he fired his revolver at the primer. The Germans were on the bridge and firing at him at this point; unfortunately the charges remained dead. He managed to make his escape, with his men, in the gathering gloom; in any case the enemy had stopped for the night and were not prepared to set off into the unknown in pursuit.

Lieutenant-Colonel Bond's KOYLI moved out of the brewery at Boussu after it had been hit by shell fire at midday and moved up towards the canal. The machine-gun officer, Lieutenant Pepys, was on the left of the St Ghislain road bridge, where he had been all day. The Battalion took up position 500 yards to the left of the road bridge and about a hundred yards south of the canal. At 2.30pm Captain Lowther took C Company up to the canal to strengthen the Borderers firing line; at about the same time Pepys was killed by a German sniper from the north bank and his place in charge of the machine-guns was taken by Lieutenant BN Denison.

The battalions of 13 Brigade were still at the canal at 6pm.[

MONDAY, 24TH: THE LAST DAY

THE FIRST HOURS

The 3rd and 5th Divisions anticipated a long battle in their new positions in Smith-Dorrien's second line; Ist

Corps also expected that it would be in a big battle on this day. Kluck had no intention of doing this, other than to engage them with enough strength to hold them; his opponents were to be swept into a trap by his manoeuvring right wing.

8 Brigade was on the right of Hamilton's 3rd Division; 4/Middx and 2/RIrR had suffered much the previous day, but they had hardly rested during the night, working instead at the trenches and defences of the new position. These men were the first beneficiaries of the new order, as Brigadier-General Doran's 8 Brigade moved south out of the salient, heading towards Bavai1.

To the right Haig's I Corps had a relatively easy time disengaging from its position. He too was cluttered with all his equipment up forward in hundreds of vehicles, carts and anything else that would carry the furnishings that go with an army on the advance. But he was able to start his move early in the morning and before the German artillery bombardment of the day had begun. He also set off towards Bavai, with 1st Division leading the way, followed two hours later by the 2nd. The route led them around the north of Maubeuge and down the very large – nine miles long by four miles wide – Mormal Forest. This feature was a major concern for all the senior commanders of the BEF, as it was inevitable that the two corps would have to pass either side of it, and they would therefore be forced apart for a significant period of time. This is not the sort of situation that forces in a withdrawing army appreciate.

On top of this straight forward topographical fact, other difficulties were considerable. Road discipline was completely absent. The limited roads available – foot-destroying pavé – were congested with French troops heading south, pathetic hordes of refugees and French

German cavalry attempting to cross by pontoon bridge are caught by British artillery.

cavalry moving across the flow, heading for the BEF's west flank. There were problems at the few bridges across the wide River Sambre; there were some clashes with German cavalry patrols; it was very difficult to keep in contact with other elements of the BEF – but, in general, the retreat went smoothly enough in the circumstances.

The six brigades of IInd Corps were fortifying their new positions, confident of their ability after seeing the German infantry convincingly repulsed in their attempts to cross the canal the previous day. True, some had managed to make it across, but at a terrible cost and at a price that prevented them following through immediately. Now the British were in positions on hills with better fields of fire and with the likelihood of more effective artillery support. Besides their feverish work, many had their first food for eighteen hours.

Smith-Dorrien received the surprising, but not altogether unwelcome, order to retire his Corps at about 4 am. However, he had the major problem of withdrawing two divisions on very limited roads, already congested with refugees, and beside the infantry there would be transport, guns and the bulk of Allenby's cavalry.

He resolved that the 3rd Division should go first; it had taken the heaviest punishment on the first day, and his left flank was the more secure. The 5th Division should be able to follow afterwards, especially as he had some support in the form of 19 Brigade and the cavalry on his left, whilst Haking's fresh 5 Brigade was on his right.

Brigadier General Doran received his orders to retire at 4.30 am, just as the German IIIrd and IXth Corps artillery began their bombardment. Fortunately the infantry had learnt their lesson well, and was leaving it to the artillery to soften the British positions. Thus the Brigade was uninterrupted as, 4/Middx leading, it slipped away from the salient without further loss.

1st Northumberland Fusiliers had worked without ceasing during the night, erecting barricades at the crossroads in the village, having taken little food and even less sleep. During the hours of darkness, when the streets should have been empty of all but soldiers, a number of civilians were found wandering the place. Spy scares were at their height, and a number were arrested, despite some pleading to be allowed to go to Cuesmes to rescue British wounded who had been left in houses there.

In the same vicinity was Brigadier General Haking's 5 Brigade. 2/Worcesters were in Frameries; to their left and slightly forward, in front of Paturages, were 2/HLI and behind and to their left were 2/Ox & Bucks and 2/CR (Connaught Rangers). They had arrived at 1 am from the reserve area of the 2nd Division near Bougnies, three miles south east of Frameries. When 2/Worcesters reached the village, not knowing what they might encounter, they had bayonets fixed and the officers had drawn their revolvers. They found it unoccupied, as the men of 9 Brigade had not then reached it. The German shelling in the early hours of the morning caused them some casualties before they, unexpectedly, withdrew.

MONS: THE LAST HOURS OF THE BATTLE

1. THE BATTLES OF FRAMERIES AND CIPLY

The fight for the hilltop village of Frameries began with the enemy's bombardment of it which started soon after dawn. It fell on the centre of the village and 2/Worcesters's position. Within an hour it lifted and with an increased ferocity was put onto 1/NF's position, moving up towards the crossroads. The enemy infantry assault started at 7.30 am when the 24th (Brandenburg) Regiment advanced to the attack from the valley dividing the village from Flenu, a mile and a half to the north.

At this critical period when Major General Hamilton's 3rd Division came under attack as it was about to move out of the salient, 9 Brigade suddenly found that its neighbour, 5 Brigade, was withdrawing without warning. This was dismaying news for Smith-Dorrien and Hamilton, but it might have been expected as it was known that Haig's I Corps (2nd Division) were already on their way out of the salient. Nevertheless, it was a blow to their plans and would later cause 13 Brigade sever problems, but at this time it was 7 and 9 Brigades that were suffering; 8 Brigade had already moved off unscathed before the battle commenced.

At the crossroads in the centre of the village, where the street ran down steeply towards Cuesmes, was A Company manning three barricades. These blockaded the roads south, east and west and had been constructed during the night by the RE and were then being strengthened by 1/NF. At the foot of the hill, straddling the road to Cuesmes, were C and D Companies and in echelon on the right was 1/Lincoln. There were four guns from 109 Battery near the railway station on the south eastern edge of the village. The Germans may well have thought that the village was empty, having seen some British troops pulling out earlier. They were to get a rude awakening when they approached the crossroads and the railway crossing at the northern edge of Frameries. Private Tebbut of 1/Lincoln later reported,

German 17th Division entering Boussu, 26 August 1914.

'I just kept firing my rifle until it got too hot to handle. At four hundred yards you could not miss and I never thought I would ever see so many dead men in such a small space.'

However, the Northumberlands and Lincolns casualties were also mounting up; both battalions slowly withdrew up the hill into the built up area. The Brandenburgers arrived at a point some hundred yards short of the barricade across the road to Cuesmes when Captain Sandilands witnessed an extraordinary incident. He was wounded, but still with his Company at the barricade, when an elderly lady approached in the midst of the mayhem. She insisted on going through the barricade to fetch a doctor to attend to the wounded who were being take into the hospital at the crossroads in the middle of the village. She could not be dissuaded, despite the bullets and flying shrapnel; she proceeded to go into a house beyond the barricade and soon reappeared with a little man carrying a black bag. No sooner had they emerged when a shell landed on the house opposite; they rushed back into the house. After a short while they came out once more, and ran back up the road to the barricade and on into the hospital.

Meanwhile the German effort had increased on the right; loud banging could be heard in the houses on the Cuesmes road as the enemy made passages through them to get at A Company.

At 8.45 am Major General Hamilton ordered Brigadier General Shaw to withdraw from the salient, increasingly concerned that otherwise his Brigade would be cut off on its left because of the withdrawal of 5 Brigade. The two battalions in Frameries began to disentangle themselves from the battle. On the left of A Company some Germans were seen attacking the western barricade fifty yards along the Paturages road. These were killed; and small rear parties kept the enemy at bay as the two battalions withdrew up the hill, en route to Eugies and Bavai. Their casualties had been considerable: 1/Lincoln had lost four officers and 134 other ranks, some of the wounded being taken prisoner in the convent hospital. Captain Ross, who was thought to have been killed, was later discovered to have been wounded and captured. 1/NF had suffered about fifty casualties, many of the wounded too badly hurt to move. A doctor, Captain M Leckie DSO, who was attached to the Northumberlands, died of his wounds in the hospital at Frameries on 28 August.

It was expected that Brigadier General McCracken's 7 Brigade at Ciply would have been able to withdraw before being attacked by the German 6th Division's attack began. Two battalions did – 2/RIRifles, which came down from the ridge a mile south of Mesvin and passed through 3/Worcesters; and the remnants of 4/RF.

2/South Lancs and 3/Worcesters in their positions on either side of main road into Cuesmes, five hundred yards south of the great, embanked railway system, had seen hundreds of Germans crossing their front since the early morning. The advance of the 24th Brandenburgers extended to this position and was met by equally effective rifle fire as they swarmed down the slope of Mount Eribus, a small hill between Ciply and Mons. The enemy was halted before they reached the triangle of railway lines and the station two hundred yards in front of 3/Worcesters' A Company.

On the left Lieutenant Colonel Wanliss' 2/South Lancs were equally under attack from the Brandenburgers; the Germans lined the railway embankment on the left, swarmed under the railway bridge and formed up behind the few houses that stood there. Facing them was D Company and Captain Travis-Cook with his machine-gun officer, Lieutenant Fulcher. They simply mowed down what they estimated to be two battalions armed with eight machine guns; they continued firing until ordered to retire. Travis-Cook, wounded seven times, finally fell with a bullet in his neck. Fulcher and his Sergeant, Harrison, shouldered the machine guns and took them away. However, a shell blew the guns off their backs and, it was feared, killed both of them. However, it was later learnt that Sergeant Harrison had not been killed but was badly wounded and taken prisoner. He was awarded the DCM and in due course served as RSM in the 5th Battalion. Fulcher was killed in November 1914 at Ypres.

Brigadier General McCracken became increasingly worried about his three battalions in the line – they should have retired long ago – and ordered them to get away as quickly as practicable and disengage from what was obviously an overwhelming force. 3/Worcesters were the first to move, covered by D Company (Captain de Salis) from a position at the railway, five hundred yards south of the sugar factory. The shell fire poured onto the escape route to the south, the Genly road, was so heavy that when it became D Company's turn the men had to retire in small sections to avoid destruction.

2/South Lancs acted as the rear guard, although 1/Wilts (Lieutenant Colonel Halstead), positioned at their road junction a mile south of Ciply and who had not been committed, would be the last to leave. As 2/South Lancs retired from the battlefield the enemy, with their machine guns on the railway embankment, raked the retreating columns of men. They had to move across the 2,000 yards of open land on either side of the Cuesmes road until they got into the shelter of the buildings on the east side of Frameries. The Battalion lost more than 300 men killed, wounded and missing – the great majority of the latter became prisoners. The RSM, Mr Robert, was found to be missing, but as happened in a large number of cases, he turned up – in this case five days and a major battle later. 3/Worcesters got off lightly with twenty-one casualties and 1/Wilts with thirty, amongst whom were Captain Dawes and Captain Rowan, the Adjutant. Halstead was fortunate to escape with only having his horse shot from under him.

The engagements at Frameries and Ciply in the four hours since the bombardment commenced and the last man retired cost 7 and 9 Brigades almost 500 casualties; but the Germans had suffered far more. Colonel von Brandis stated that he had lost three company commanders, every second officer, every third man;

Captain Liebenow of the 64th Regiment said that his Battalion had lost every fourth man and every lieutenant. The total German casualties were over a thousand, all dead or wounded; over half those of the British were prisoners, though many were wounded.

The Germans, crossing the Condé Canal at both its east and west ends, could now turn their attention to the left of the British line south of the canal. There seemed that there was still the prospect of driving Smith-Dorrien's IInd Corps into the trap of Maubeuge.

THE BATTLE AT WASMES

Essentially this battle involved 13 Brigade, with the addition of part of 1/Dorset from 14 Brigade. When the battalions were withdrawn in the very early hours of Monday morning, it was in the confident expectation that they were going into positions from where they could hold the enemy off for as long as need be. Their casualties thus far had not been heavy and they knew that they had inflicted a very heavy toll on the enemy in his attempts to cross the canal.

The village was packed with troops from the Brigade. 2/Duke of Wellington's were dug in on an arc a mile long around the northern edge, its peak at the crossroad a thousand yards to the north west of the village square at a point called La Justice. 500 yards east on the Binche road was an area known as Le Bosquet; 500 yards further to the east was D Company, at a large slag heap which marked the limit of the Battalion's right flank. On the left were three companies (A, B, C) of 1/Dorsets. They looked down the slope to Hornu, a thousand yards to the north; south of

'I bayoneted a German, but before I could withdraw it I was clubbed on the head with a rifle.'

An artist impression of a British bayonet charge in process at Mons.

them, on the western perimeter of the Wasmes defences, was B Company (Major CG Pack-Beresford) of 1/RWK. Elements of all three battalions were inside the village perimeter, whilst the KOYLIs were in Paturages, to the south.

Until about 11 am the Germans contented themselves with bombarding Wasmes and the various positions of the infantry. Although Frameries had long since fallen, they were in no hurry to lose more men than they needed. They were content to hold the Brigade whilst the threatening sweep from the right developed.

Major General Fergusson gave the order for 14 Brigade to retire from the salient towards Bavai, to be followed by the 13th, which he knew would cover the former's withdrawal. They would be followed by 15 Brigade, which would cover the rear of the 5th Division. In turn, they would be followed by Allenby's cavalry and 19 Brigade. The salient was to be empty of British troops by the early afternoon. However, almost as soon as the order was given, Fergusson learnt that Allenby's cavalry had already gone, unable to find any signs of a great German advance, at 8 am. Drummond had withdrawn his 19 Brigade for the same reason. Smith-Dorrien's left flank was 'in the air'; the 5th Division had a long way to go before it could be clear.

To make matters worse, the Germans began to attack Wasmes in strength; and the 8th Division began to drive through Crespin to cut off the exodus of IInd Corps.

Fergusson asked Allenby to stop his withdrawal if he could and give some support to his left flank. He then formed a 'task force' from 15 Brigade to act as a left flank shield until he could extract 13 Brigade from the fighting at Wasmes; finally the 15th could move out – what was left of it, as 1/Dorset was fighting with 13 Brigade and 1/Bedfords with 14 Brigade, and these units would withdraw with them.

Before midday the German infantry had advanced against Wasmes in great strength. On the right flank was No. 12 Platoon of C Company, 2/Duke of Wellington's, who could see the enemy coming across a corn field carrying stooks as shields. Lieutenant LE Russel was down to twelve men (he had started with thirty). He ordered them to fix bayonets and to empty their magazines into the advancing Germans. They then stood up and charged into their foe, fighting a bitter hand to hand battle until all the Dukes had been killed. A platoon of D Company was near them; its commander, Sergeant Spence, ordered his men to fix bayonets and fight their way back into the village centre. A survivor, Corporal Williams, wrote;

> '*The bodies of Germans were piled up all around. I bayoneted a German, but before I could withdraw it I was clubbed on the head with a rifle, knocked out and became a prisoner.*'

Williams had been previously wounded in the foot. Lieutenant Colonel Gibbs, lying badly wounded and soon to be made prisoner, saw Sergeant Spence – also seriously wounded – gather his handful of men together and charge up the street near the church. They cleared the street, the Germans fleeing from the shouting, cursing men coming up the road at them, which enabled two platoons to retire. Spence earned a DCM for his actions, but was made prisoner.

At 4 pm the battle continued, but the village was invested by the enemy, with hand to hand fighting taking place amongst the winding narrow streets and the many slag heaps that were such a feature of the landscape here. On the left flank the battle had been no less intense. Major Pack Beresford, Captain Phillips and Lieutenant Broadwood of 1/RWK and many of their men were killed. The Dorsets gradually fell back south of the railway running through Wasmes. By 4.30 pm the Germans had removed any possibility of the men still in the village escaping capture. The casualties were high. 1/Dorsets lost three officers wounded and taken prisoner and 132 other ranks casualties; 1/RWK five oficers and twenty other ranks; but it was 2/Duke of Wellington's that suffered the most. The Adjutant, Major PB Stafford, Captain Denham-Jubb and Lieutenant Russel were killed; four other officers were wounded and captured, including the CO, whilst Lieutenant Thompson was to die of his wounds on 14 September. Captain Jenkins and Lieutenant Price were missing and 316 other ranks were casualties. The holding action at Wasmes had cost almost five hundred casualties.

The Royal Artillery had also suffered losses – including Major CS Holland, who commanded 120 Battery. For the most part, however, the guns were got out by midday and were able to play their vital part in the retreat.

The Belgians had helped as much as they could with the wounded. Captain Taylor (2/Duke of Wellington's) was wounded and was then taken into hiding by the Barbier family. In September he felt fit enough to make a run for home (it should be borne in mind that there was far from being anything resembling a solid line between the opposing armies at this stage in the war – that would not come to pass until November). Madam Barbier found him some clothes, money and provisions and also found a reliable man to act as his guide. The Captain set off, taking a large suitcase with him in which was his uniform, so that he could put it on if the situations arose and prove that he was not a spy. He alternately walked and hid through an area that was filled with Germans. He succeeded in making it to the small town of Peruwelz, fifteen miles to the north west of Wasmes and managed to catch the last train to Tournai and Ostend.

Captain Ellis and fifty men (also 2/Duke of Wellington's) were cut off in a wood; in the various encounters with the enemy the group was scattered until Ellis and Corporal Kerman were the only ones left. Still wearing their uniform, for twelve days they walked south at night and hid by day as they were amongst the advancing German army. Eventually a man found them and took them to a priest's house. The priest took them to a Belgian man who had worked in London to act as their guide. Armed with a card from the priest, asking all who could to help them, the two (now dressed in civilian clothes) with their guide set off. On the way they picked up two men from the Manchesters, and continuing their cat and mouse act with the Germans, they eventually made it through to Leuze, some thirty miles from where they had started. There they caught a train to Ostend and boarded a British destroyer, which took them to England, arriving there on 5 September. They returned to France in due course and rejoined their Battalion. The two officers from 2/DoW who escaped were to be killed on Hill 60, near Ypres, on 18 April 1915.

THE BATTLE AT AUDREGNIES: THE GLORIOUS LAST STAND OF THE 1ST CHESHIRE REGIMENT (22ND OF FOOT).

The left flank guard of the 5th Division consisted of 1/Norfolk (Lieutenant Colonel CR Ballard) and 1/Cheshires (Lieutenant Colonel DC Boger). With the two battalions was Major Alexander's 119 Field Battery and Brigadier General de Lisle's 2 (Cavalry) Brigade: 4/DG, 9/Lancers and 18/Hussars. The Dragoons and Lancers took up positions on the left flank, on the western side of the small hill top village of Audregnies and looking out to the north. Allenby also sent them Major Sclater Booth's L battery of the RHA (Royal Horse Artillery). Ballard, the senior officer, commanded the small force. They began to get into place at 11 am; facing them, not more than 3,000 yards away, were 5,000 German infantry approaching quickly from the left, from Quievrain, whilst at a similar distance 2,000 men were advancing from Thulin, to the north. Only 5,000 yards away there were nine batteries of artillery and a further fifteen battalions of infantry coming up behind this force. This was an overwhelming force, the sharp end of von Kluck's scythe that was to drive Smith-Dorrien's IInd Corps into Maubeuge. The British had a real fight on their hands.

The position at Audregnies was a good one. The German line of attack had to come across fairly level, low-lying and open ground to a ridge running north east from Audregnies towards Elouges, two miles away. The fields were scarred by coal mine workings, and the main railway line ran across them from the south east to the north west. There was a minor railway line that ran from a spoil heap in the middle of the German attack line and yet another main line from Mons ran through the south edge of Audregnies. On the left flank, coming out of Audregnies, a pavéd, narrow Roman road ran perfectly straight towards Quievrain and beyond. Some 2,000 yards along it was a sugar factory, a collection of brick buildings on either side of the road. From there two roads branched to the left, forming a letter V. Initially the 72nd Regiment would attack across and down either side of it.

The two batteries positioned themselves behind the ridge top road from Elouges to Angre, a village a mile and a half south west of Audregnies; Major Alexander's

119 Battery took the right flank, near the mineral railway and L Battery the left, in the low ground behind Audregnies. The two cavalry regiments that took part in the action were in the hollow behind Audregnies at the beginning of the Roman road – 9/Lancers on the right and 4/DG on the left. Their subsequent full-blooded charge would be the first such made by the British during the war. One other cavalry regiment would see significant action this day, when the Germans, frustrated by the flank guard, tried to get around it by coming through the hamlet of Marchipont. They were stopped by 5/DG [1 (Cavalry) Brigade] and D and E Batteries RHA.

A rest period during the retreat from Mons.

At 11.30 am Lieutenant Colonel Ballard began to place his Battalion in position. They were spread out along a track that ran parallel to the main road from Elouges, 800 yards north of it and crossed the main railway line. Lieutenant Colonel Boger deployed in a similar fashion, dividing the line from the left flank of the Norfolks to Audregnies (about a mile) between his companies. They were behind the main road, with some of the platoons following the same track as the Norfolks, which came gradually closer to the main road until they joined two hundred yards north of the village. He put his two machine-guns in a deserted cottage on the bend at this road junction; they had an excellent view over the ground and the Roman road before them. The major landmarks to their north were a windmill a few hundred yards ahead and the sugar factory well beyond it.

The men had no time to dig trenches but made use of ditches and hollows, making them deeper if they could. Because the road undulated, no company could see another. At a few minutes after midday the German artillery began its bombardment; the British replied as the German infantry advanced on a 5,000 yard line.

Almost immediately the Cheshires suffered their first casualty. CSM Meachin (of Captain Shore's B Company) was struck in the head by a bullet as he went to his position on Farm House, some 200 yards down the road from the machine guns' position. Beyond C Company were, in order, A (Captain Dyer), C (Captain Dugmore) and out on the right, D (Captain Jones) – the extreme part of which was commanded by Captain Rich, whose men were spaced out at five pace intervals. Jones would be killed and Dyer and Dugmore wounded during the day's fighting. The Cheshires were taking casualties from the artillery (Lieutenant Bolton and Private Thorpe hit by shell splinters) before they had even fired a shot in reply.

Lieutenant Randall, commanding the machine-gun section, was the first to open fire; setting the guns range at 1,800 yards he opened up on German aircraft hovering over the British position. They were too high to be dealt with by such fire, and the Germans obviously registered their location, for all too quickly one of the guns was hit and put out of action.

The Norfolks received the same sort of treatment. A platoon that was perilously positioned forward of the spoil heap (marked 'collieries' on the map) between the railway line and the main road was in danger of being cut off. The Battalion soon lost two officers killed, Captain Cresswell followed by the Second in Command, Major JB Orr.

Boger then advanced some of his men further forward towards a sunken road that crossed the Roman road, so that they could get to a better range. Enemy shelling increased, now from a range of only 2,000 yards, and Captain Jackson was badly wounded (he was captured where he fell) and one of his sergeants, Walden, was killed.

Because of the lack of visual contact, Dugmore sent men to make contact with other companies and Battalion Headquarters in the village – none returned. The tremendous volume of fire falling on the road almost precluded movement. CQMS Pitt (D Company) saw a section of 119 Battery galloping furiously down the road to go into position behind the company, but it received the full force of a shell, piling men, horses, limber and 18 pdr into a broken mass on the road. With the Cheshires mules madly stampeding, the scene was of utter confusion and mayhem, to which was added flying shrapnel and bullets.

Fortunately the Germans chose to advance in the same reckless fashion so often employed in the battles in and around Mons – en masse and firing from the hip, with only an accidental chance of actually hitting someone. A captain of the Norfolks arrived with some reinforcements for D Company, but the shelling was so heavy that they had to take up position behind the railway embankment. Two German regiments, the 72nd and 26th, were now coming in close order behind the barrage, and were heading straight for the forward elements of the two battalions between the Roman road and the curving railway line.

It was now about 1 pm. Brigadier General de Lisle, seeing the serious situation facing the Cheshires, ordered his cavalry forward. There was to follow one of the bravest of cavalry charges, one of the epic moments of the war. Two squadrons of 9/Lancers, led by Lieutenant Colonel Campbell along with Captain Lucas Tooth and Captain FO Grenfall, charged up the right hand side of the Roman road, jumping the deeply sunken road crossing it a thousand yards ahead. Meanwhile two troops of 4/DG attacked up the left hand side of the road, led by Lieutenant Colonel Mullens and Major Tom Bridges; the latter had been involved in the first British cavalry charge of the war. Nothing then was more fear inspiring than 400 men mounted on horses, armed with lances and sabres, yelling and screaming in a mad charge towards you. A vague idea can be obtained by standing on the Mall in front of the Household Cavalry as they move to or from their public duties – one is more than happy to get out of the way as the sheer size of the force approaches.

Spearing or cutting down all who got in their way they raced closer to the sugar factory, scattering the terrified infantry, who had seen nothing like it, but losing men and horses all the time from the batteries of artillery, firing point blank at them, and from machine guns. The cavalry had met its historic fate with the advent of numerous machine guns, but it still had an important role to play in the war – there was no other land means of transport that could move so quickly and with such versatility during the whole of the conflict; whilst Flowerdew was to lead a full scale cavalry charge as late as spring 1918 against defended positions with vital consequences for a battle.

On the left of the Roman road Major Bridges was one of the first to go down, his horse shot from under him. Kicked in the face and unconscious, he was rescued by two RAMC men and taken to a cottage on the edge of Baisieux, 500 yards from where he had fallen. When he came round he looked through the window and saw lines of German infantry marching towards the village. He climbed through a window at the rear and found a wounded horse and made his way to Audregnies. He was deprived of speech by the blow in his face and was still disoriented and so sat down by the side of the road. Some time later he saw, to his complete disbelief, a blue and silver Rolls Royce being driven by an officer, 'having a look round'. The Major got aboard and was whisked away, thereby avoiding certain capture. He survived to become a lieutenant general, a knight and to have a chestful of decorations.

The Dragoons' charge was brought to a halt in front of the sugar factory – a charge whose cost was awful. 9/Lancers suffered similarly heavy casualties. On approaching the sugar factory they found that barbed wire divided the fields there, leaving them no alternative but to swerve to the right in front of the German guns massed in the area. The three officers (all wounded) with the survivors and riderless horses raced along the south

edge of the railway embankment towards the spoil heap workings and main road, where the British infantry lines were. The Colonel and his few remaining men dismounted and fought with the Norfolks' platoon at the workings. Grenfell, still on his wounded horse, found shelter under the embankment. Campbell wanted to get fresh orders and so left Lucas Tooth in command and galloped across open ground and through the hail of steel to see de Lisle. Captain Lucas Tooth remained fighting with the infantry but eventually withdrew his men; his actions that day won him the DSO, but he was to be killed on the Aisne. The cavalry lost about 300 horses and 250 casualties in their day's fighting.

Captain Grenfell was not yet finished with the battle, however. He tried to return to his squadron, which was a mile away, on the other side of Audregnies. He came to Major Alexander's 119 Battery, which had been ordered to withdraw because of the proximity of the enemy. Only Major Alexander remained amongst the officers and some two dozen men, most of whom were wounded. There were no horses remaining. Grenfell walked his horse through the storm of steel to see where the guns had to be taken. On his return, on the track to Wiheries, he found a number of his officer comrades and returned with them. The total number at the battery was now forty and the four guns were manhandled over the fields until they reached the Elouges to Wiheries road, some 1400 yards away. Wounded again, Grenfell stayed with the battery until it was safely away from the action. Both he and Major Alexander were awarded the Victoria Cross and Sergeants Davids and Turner won the DCM. Grenfell was killed at Ypres nine months later; other members of his family killed in the war included his twin brother, and two of his cousins. His elder brother had been killed at Omdurman and another cousin in the Boer War. The military history and sacrifice of the Grenfall family is quite remarkable. Another member of the family was the outstanding comedienne, Joyce Grenfall.

The time was now about 4 pm. Boger's orders had been to hold on at all costs, and this is what he had achieved thus far. The Germans had got through his forward defences and were close to the road. He could see the Germans massing for a second assault on the left, coming out of Bois du Deduit, south of Quievrain. This was the 93rd Regiment whilst to the north, on his right flank, the 66th Regiment were fast approaching. Boger sent a cyclist to Lieutenant Colonel Ballard for his view of the situation – and then three more – but none of them returned. Similarly, Ballard had sent him three messages, informing the Cheshires that as the last of IInd Corps had withdrawn he was about to retire, and so should the Cheshires. None of these messages got through.

1/Norfolk retired. They had lost three officers killed, four wounded and 250 other ranks of whom a hundred

> 'On the left of the Roman road Major Bridges was one of the first to go down, his horse shot from under him.'

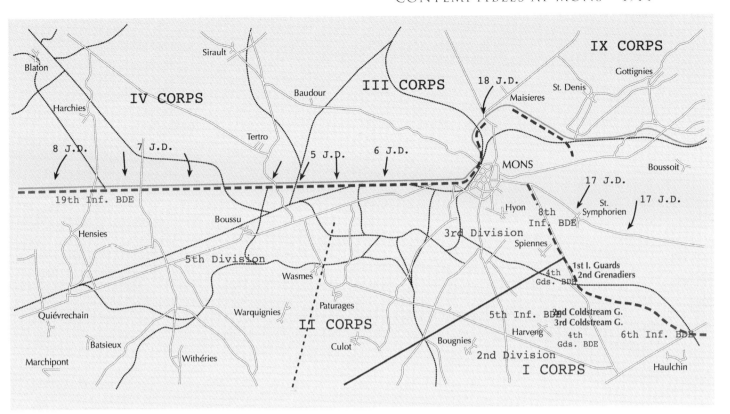

THE BATTLE OF MONS – 23 AUGUST 1914

had been left behind at Elouges, too badly wounded to be moved. Some of the Battalion was left behind with the Cheshires, near the spoil heap, as they had got detached from their own men and never received the order to pull out.

Boger's Battalion, did he but know it, was very much on its own. The cavalry had withdrawn after their fight at Marchipoint and L Battery had gone with them.

Both flanks of the Cheshires came under increasingly heavy pressure. Lieutenants Matterson (Scout Officer) and Campbell of B Company, who could see the pressure on A Company coming from the other side of the Roman road, took some reinforcements towards it; Campbell was killed almost instantly. The Battalion was now gradually being pushed in towards the village, with the enemy seemingly everywhere. Captain Dugmore, with eight men, retired to the small bridge at the light railway and put up their final resistance. Private Rich of B Company with some of his men and Sergeant Blackwell and a few Norfolks still at the colliery, fell back, with every man for himself.

A Company, on the track running north east of Audregnies towards the spoil heap, was about to retire when two machine guns began to fire on them. Captains Dyer, Joliffe and Massey, Lieutenant Matterson and about thirty men, with bayonets already fixed, charged them; in doing so they hoped to give the remaining men a chance to get away. They actually got more than 500 yards, the Germans melting away from them as they charged. Dyer, Massey and Joliffe were wounded and lay where they fell, with only some ten men surviving. Lieutenant Elliott of A Company rushed forward to pick up a wounded man, Private Miller, from the road, but

was shot in both feet. Elliott managed to crawl to a deserted cottage and hid – in fact the occupants were hiding down a well. When the Germans found him and demanded his sword, he refused to surrender it; Leutnant Rogge (himself subsequently killed) of the 72nd Regiment told him to keep it.

Wounded British cavalrymen in retreat.

61

Boger, seeing that his position was enveloped on both sides, ordered his men to retire to Audregnies Wood. At this time he was shot in the foot and in the right side.

Captain ER Jones saw some men of C Company pulling back from the main road; he gathered them to an embankment where there was better cover. They had to pull back still further, into the edge of the wood, soon after. He had about a dozen men with him, two of whom were young drummers. Coming across some Germans hiding behind corn stooks he opened fire with his revolver; both he and Drummer Hogan were killed instantly, and two others were mortally wounded. The long battle was nearly over.

Captain Shore (the only Captain left) with part of B Company were seen by a staff officer when they left the farm house they were holding because it was rapidly being destroyed. The staff officer gave orders that they were to go to the rear, where the two battalions were reforming. They kept going until they met up with the Norfolks; they were the only formed party of Cheshires to escape capture.

The time was now after 5 pm and the shelling ceased, because the German infantry had penetrated the Cheshires defensive perimeter almost everywhere and had got, in places, onto the main road. Lieutenant Colonel Boger lay in a field close to the road from Audregnies to Wiheries, unable to move. All about him were his dead and wounded men, but small parties were still fighting all over the battlefield and within the village and wood. At 6 pm all fighting had ceased and the surviving Cheshires rounded up as prisoners, though some hundreds of wounded were left where they had fallen and would have to stay there for some time before help came to them.

Some Germans came across the wounded Colonel and the group of wounded near him and took his revolver and binoculars and broke the men's rifles; but left them where they were. In the dark Boger heard a man calling faintly in the distance and crawled over to the spot, finding Sergeant Dowling, who had both his legs smashed. Some time later a German officer found Boger and had him carried into a cottage; and shortly afterwards he was joined there by Dowling and both men were treated by a doctor. Dowling died as a prisoner in 1917.

1/Cheshire had done more than could have been expected of them and had done more than anyone to defy the attempt of von Kluck's IVth Corps to surround the BEF; they had served to halt the great drive of the 7th and 8th Divisions to the south. The Germans found it difficult to believe that their tremendous casualties had been caused by a few riflemen and vigorously demanded to know where they had hidden the machine guns, as they were sure there must have been many deployed against them. The salient was at last quiet.

That night a roll call was taken in a valley at St Wast, three miles north of Bavai, of those who had got away. Out of 1,007 men and 27 officers who had taken part in the battle at Audregnies, only 192 men and 6 officers

were able to answer their names. Lieutenant Colonel Boger's Battalion had been destroyed, but as with so many others during those first months of the war, was soon reformed and 1/Cheshire became once again a fighting force. Its new commander, Lieutenant Colonel Vandaleur, was himself seriously wounded near Bethune, captured, but then escaped back to England.

Field Marshal Sir John French's BEF had gone to Mons expecting to take part in an advance; instead they had been forced to fight a two day defensive battle. The German casualties, even when compared with some of the great battles of later in the war, were staggering. In the Battle of Mons proper, on 23 August, the British had lost over 1,600. On the second day, with the unexpected change in plans from a defensive stand to a hasty withdrawal, there were about a thousand casualties; except that on the left flank, the most vulnerable part of the operation, there were a further fifteen hundred from two battalions, some three squadrons of cavalry, a couple of batteries of artillery and some sappers. The grand total of 4,150 could be compared with the losses of, say, the 7th Division in First Ypres. In eighteen days this formation lost 356 officers and 9,644 other ranks, out of a total of 12,400 who had taken the field.

In the battle of the Mons salient six Victoria Crosses were won.

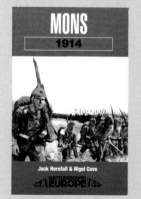

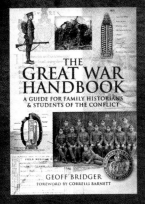

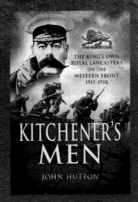

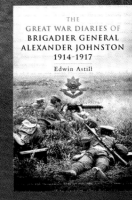

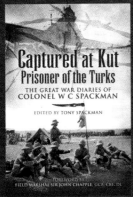

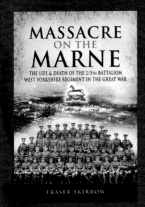
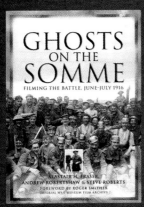

LE CATEAU –
A HISTORY AND A GUIDE

Following its defeat at Mons on 23 August 1914 the BEF fell back to the south, pursued by the Germans. Just after dawn three confused days later, on the anniversary of the Battle of Crécy, von Kluck's army caught Smith-Dorrien's tired II Corps at le Cateau from where, after a morning's battle, the retreat continued. British casualties were about 8,000 men and 38 guns. German casualties are estimated at 9,000.

By Tonie & Valmai Holt

Extracted from *Major and Mrs Holt's Battlefield Guide to The Western Front – North* and reproduced by permission of Pen & Sword Books Ltd.

'Early on that memorable day the Cornwalls, after a wretched night, stood to arms.
It was still dark and their clothes were sodden with rain: many had not slept at all. Stand To was the worst hour of the day: chilled through and drowsy.'
DCLI Regimental History.

'When men are too tired to march, they must lie down and fight.'
Gen Sir Horace Smith-Dorrien, GCB, DSO, Commanding II Corps.

OPENING MOVES

The plan of the French Commander-in-Chief, General Joffre, to counter the German invasion was known as 'Plan 17'. Its essential idea was that of a massive counter-attack through the German centre to the south-east of Belgium. What came out of Plan 17 was a series of four major engagements known as 'The Battle of the Frontiers'.

In three of the battles in Lorraine, the Ardennes and on the Sambre, the French, following their tactical doctrine of *l'attaque à l'outrance* (attack to the extreme), threw themselves forward into the maelstrom of German machine-gun and artillery fire without apparent regard to tactical caution.

The French offensive stopped in bloody confusion with over 300,000 casualties and the armies began to withdraw.

The fourth 'Battle of the Frontiers' was the stand of the BEF at Mons on 23 August and as night fell Sir John French, the British Commander-in-Chief, had in mind to continue the defence the following day.

The French 5th Army to the immediate right of the BEF was under the command of the 62-year-old General Lanrézac who, believing that the security of his whole army was threatened, that same night of 23 August gave the order for a general retreat without telling Joffre – or the BEF. Fortunately there was a British liaison officer with the 5th Army who brought the news of the withdrawal to Sir John in his HQ at le Cateau just before midnight. Orders were sent immediately for the BEF to retire.

General Haig's I Corps, which had not been in action, received its orders by wire at 0200 hours on 24 August and was underway before dawn. General Smith-Dorrien's II Corps HQ was not in telegraphic contact, having been in battle all day at Mons, and its orders did not arrive until 0300 hours. As II Corps began to move it was once more under fire.

Sir John French oscillated between innocent optimism and extreme pessimism about the military situation. The British High Command did not trust the French and Lanrézac's retreat reinforced that attitude. When Lord Kitchener had briefed the British C-in-C on the responsibilities of the BEF he had said that it was 'to support and co-operate with the French Army' but had added 'You will in no case come in any sense under the orders of any allied general'. Sir John had met Lanrézac on 17 August, a week before Mons. Neither spoke the other's language and the meeting ended uncomfortably. Thus nation to nation there was hardly accord in the adjoining allied forces.

Yet things were just as bad within the BEF. Douglas Haig, commanding I Corps under Sir John, wrote in his diary, 'I know that (Sir John) French is quite unfit for this great command', while Sir John was not at all pleased at the appointment of Horace Smith-Dorrien to command II Corps. He had named General Plumer to take over after the original Corps commander died, but Kitchener chose Smith-Dorrien, who himself wasn't the greatest fan of the C-in-C. These antipathies laid reins over the course of the coming battle and led to unpleasant post-war altercations as to whether the battle of le Cateau need ever have been fought.

At 2025 hours on 24 August Sir John French issued 'Operation Order No. 7'. It said in part:

'The army will move tomorrow, 25th inst, to a position in the neighbourhood of le Cateau, exact positions will be pointed out on the ground tomorrow.'

It was a long march. I Corps was to take the eastern half of the position and II Corps the western. On average the troops had to march between 20 and 25 miles. I Corps routes were very complex, crossing and recrossing the River Sambre, and they were also occupied here and there by the retreating French. Thus I Corps fell behind II Corps and communication between the Corps was lost.

At 2100 hours on 25 August Smith-Dorrien received orders from GHQ to continue the withdrawal on the following day and not to make a stand. Yet II Corps actually stood and fought. The reader is invited to consider the circumstances in which the decision to fight was made and for that purpose should now assume the identity of General Smith-Dorrien. Imagine that it is 0200 hours on the morning of 26 August. Your Corps has been on the move for 24 hours, marching along roads thick with refugees. It is dark. It is raining. You have no communications with I Corps but you have heard rumours that they are behind (to the north) of you and that they are under pressure from the Germans.

Your troops are tired and are now approaching the town of le Cateau, which offers a certain solidity for defence and some comfort from the elements. You may get an idea of the conditions from this account by Frank Richards, a soldier in the Royal Welch Fusiliers, who described in *Old Soldiers Never Die* how he got to the town from Mons:

> 'We marched all night and the greatest part of the next day and dug trenches. We were only in those trenches a few hours before we were on the march again... We marched all night again and all next day. We arrived in le Cateau about midnight, dead-beat to the world. I don't believe any one of us at this time realised that we were retiring, though it was clear that we were not going in the direction of Germany. Of course the officers knew, but they were telling us that we were drawing the enemy into a trap. Le Cateau that night presented a strange sight. Everyone was in a panic, packing up their stuff on carts and barrows to get away south in time. The Royal Welch camped on the square in the centre of the town. We were told to get as much rest as we could. The majority sank down where they were and fell straight asleep.'

General Allenby suddenly arrives at your HQ and says, in effect, 'The high ground before le Cateau that I planned to hold to cover your retreat tomorrow has been taken by the enemy. I cannot contact General French and in my opinion the Germans will attack you at first light unless you can get away now and in the dark.' You are also out of contact with GHQ which has moved back to St Quentin. It is up to you alone to decide what to do. You call in your divisional commanders to report to you. They virtually say, 'Many men are separated from their units', or 'The men are too weary to move before the morning', or 'The roads are jammed

with refugees', or 'Some roads have been washed out by the storm.'

What would you decide to do? Would you obey your order to continue to retreat? Smith-Dorrien decided to disobey his orders and to stay and fight on the ridge which runs behind the town and roughly parallel to the le Cateau-Cambrai road.

WHAT HAPPENED

Shortly after dawn on 26 August, German troops of the left hand column of III (Ger) Corps entered le Cateau and came up against elements of 5th Division – the Duke of Cornwall's Light Infantry (DCLI) and East Surreys – near the railway bridge, when after a short fire fight conducted from the windows of the houses the British withdrew to the high ground behind the town.

Realising that the British meant to stand and fight, von Kluck decided to mount a frontal attack with IV (Ger) Corps behind an artillery barrage on the main British line behind the Cambrai-le Cateau road, and to send III (Ger) Corps to the east to outflank the BEF (see **Map**). The British line consisted of 5th Division on the high ground astride the Roman road covering from le Cateau to Troisvilles, 3rd Division to the west up to Caudry and the newly arrived 4th Division beyond that.

An early German cavalry attack on the extreme left of the BEF was checked and German small arms activity then focused upon the 5th Division area through the morning, with infantry pressing forward tactically across the broken ground with machine guns, and using the spire of le Cateau church as an Observation Point (OP). By mid-morning the Germans controlled the high ground to the east of the River Selle and had uncovered the end of the British position.

The morning had been an artillery battle above all else, with some 230 Royal Artillery pieces ranged against about 550 of the enemy along the total frontage of about 13 miles. The 5th Division area from the le Cateau spur to Troisvilles was about 4½ miles and consisted mostly of cut cornfields with patches of beet and clover, dramatically different to the houses and slag heaps of Mons. With the exception of the broken ground behind the railway station the general aspect was one of gently rolling Atlantic waves of open fields. There was little opportunity to find cover for guns or for men.

The Germans continued to concentrate their efforts upon the le Cateau spur across which the Roman road struck straight through to St Quentin. A breakthrough at le Cateau could divide and perhaps destroy Smith-Dorrien's Corps. The main strain of the attack fell upon the King's Own Yorkshire Light Infantry (KOYLI) and the Suffolks and an attempt to reinforce them by the Manchesters and two companies of the Argylls failed. Nevertheless, at midday the British line still held.

Inexorably von Kluck's forces built up against the open right flank and by 1300 hours the British on the

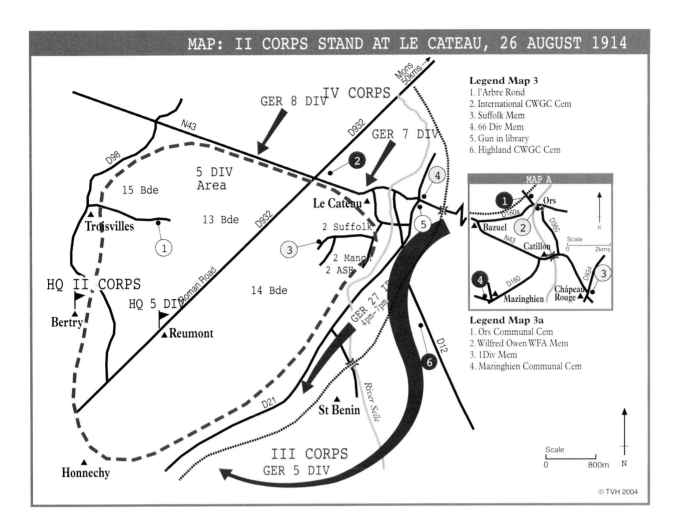

exposed spur were under artillery fire from three German divisions and under frontal and flank attacks by a dozen infantry battalions. It was time to get out.

Smith-Dorrien decided to withdraw by divisions from right to left, i.e. 5th Division would be the first to move. His order was issued at 1340 hours but much of the line communication had been destroyed by the artillery bombardments and the message had to be delivered by runner. 5th Division HQ received the order at 1400 hours, forward units got it at 1500 hours. 2nd KOYLI and 2nd Suffolk never got it at all and by 1600 hours they were surrounded and wiped out.

The Royal Artillery had suffered badly. Not a single Battery left on the ridge was capable of sustained action, being damaged or without horses or ammunition. But some guns could be saved – *had* to be saved – and, in volunteering to return to the ridge and recover the remaining two guns of 37 (Howitzer) Battery, **Drivers Fred Luke and Job Drain, as well as their officer, Captain Douglas Reynolds, won the VC.** Luke survived to serve with the RAF Regt in WW2. Drain also survived and formed part of the Honour Guard at the burial of the Unknown Soldier at Westminster Abbey on 11 November 1920. Both he and Luke attended the VC Reunion Dinner given at the House of Lords on 9 November 1929. On 9 September Reynolds silenced a battery which he had

discovered while reconnoitring, was severely wounded on 15 September and killed at Le Touquet on 23 February 1916. He is buried in Etaples Mil Cemetery.

Thus II Corps withdrew from le Cateau, having stopped the German advance for half a day in a battle that many, including Sir John French, said should never have been fought. Others believed that the fight had saved the BEF and even the C-in-C in his Despatch dated 7 September 1914 wrote, 'I cannot close the brief account of this glorious stand of the British troops without putting on record my deep appreciation of the valuable services rendered by General Sir Horace Smith-Dorrien. I say without hesitation, that the saving of the left wing of the Army under my command on the morning of August 26 could never have been accomplished unless a commander of rare and unusual coolness, intrepidity and determination had been present to conduct the operation personally.'

Later French was to vilify the II Corps Commander (who was extremely popular with his men and whose cheery smile was recorded as being a great morale-raising factor during the Retreat) and accuse him of disobeying orders at le Cateau. In 1915 he had Smith-Dorrien recalled to England.

However, contact with the Germans had been broken. They did not immediately pursue and the BEF was able to breathe a little more easily as it fell back towards Paris and the Marne. Le Cateau cost over 8,000 casualties and 38 guns.

THE BATTLEFIELD TOUR

- **The Route:** The tour begins near the 'Arbre Rond', then visits the International Cemetery, continues through le Cateau to the 66th Div Commemorative Horse Trough. It then visits Ors on the Sambre-Oise Canal where the poet Wilfred Owen was killed – his grave in the CWGC Comm Cem and the WFA Memorial; the 1st Div Memorial at La Groise; the Highland Cemetery and the Suffolk Memorial on the le Cateau Ridge.
- **Extra Visit** to 5th Div Battle HQ, Reumont.
- **Total distance:** 27.9 miles
- **Total time:** 2 hours 30 minutes
- **Distance to Calais from start point** via Cambrai: 105 miles. Motorway Tolls
- **Base town:** Cambrai
- **Map:** IGN 2607 Est Le Cateau 1:25,000 and 2707

L'Abre Rond.

From Calais take the A26/E15 and then the E17 to the junction with the E19/A2. Take the Cambrai direction and come off at Exit 14 on the N30. Follow signs to Cambrai Centre then follow signs to Valenciennes around the town and pick up signs to F[aubour]g du Cateau and then le Cateau on the N43. Continue through Beaumont.

As the Roman road rises to a crest after Inchy you are effectively in No Man's Land with the German assaults coming from your left towards 5th Division positions on your right.

Turn right just before the restaurant 'Le Pendu' on the D98. Set your mileometer to 0. Continue to Troisvilles to the large calvary in the village. Keep left and continue to a crossroads with another calvary.

N.B. In the **Troisvilles Communal Cemetery** ahead are 30 British WW1 burials, over half of whom are Unknown and which include 5 Special Memorials to men who fell on 26 August 1914. The cemetery was first used by the Germans in August 1914 and by British units in 1918.

Turn left along a track which is driveable if reasonably dry. Continue to the lone tree to the right of the electricity pylons.

- **L'ARBRE ROND/1.7 MILES/5 MINUTES/MAP/1**
This is Point 138, l'Arbre Rond, on the IGN map. At the time of the battle trees were few and far between in the area and the tree that stood here was about 40 ft high. It was marked on the maps that the Germans had and they used the tree as a marker on which to range their artillery.

The 15th Brigade of 5th Division held this area with Brigade HQ nearby in the cutting. The 1st Norfolks were tasked to prepare the defences – and they wanted the tree down so that the German guns could not range upon it. They set about sawing it through but never quite finished the job.

There are various accounts about the fate of the tree and the reported planting of a sapling in the late 1950s, but the romantic can scrutinize the gnarled trunk and be convinced that healed saw cuts can still be discerned.

Return to the N43 and turn right. Continue to the crossroads and turn left signed to le Cateau Mil and German Cemetery. Continue to the cemetery on the right.

- **LE CATEAU CWGC INTERNATIONAL MILITARY AND GERMAN CEMETERIES/5.4 MILES/ 20 MINUTES/MAP/2**
This is also known as the International Cemetery because of the considerable number of British, German and Russian burials. The ground was laid out by the Germans in February 1916 with plots for their own and for the British dead which have separate entrances and visitors' books. There are over 5,000 Germans buried here (most in a mass grave) including some females. There are a number of large German memorials including a pyramid structure on which is embossed *See Getreu bis den Tod* (Faithful unto Death). Curiously a very similar pyramid is to be found on the 1942 battlefield of El Alamein to commemorate German fighter pilot Captain H. J. Marseille. Also in this cemetery is a memorial column erected by the Leibkurassier Regiment which names its casualties on the day of the battle. Thirty-four Russian prisoners lie together in a separate plot.

The British burials number some 640, buried in sections representative of 1914 and 1918 and include 3 UK Navy, 473 UK Army, 1 UK Airforce and 182 Unknown, 6 Australians, 2 Canadians and 1 Unknown, 2 New Zealanders, 24 South African and 4 Unknown and 2 German. The CWGC Plots were designed by Charles Holden. There is also a French

German Pyramid Memorial, International Cemetery, le Cateau.

Headstone of L/Cpl Sayer, VC.

plot at the back which is not listed in the Cemetery Report.

Here is buried **Lance Corporal John William Sayer, VC**, 8th Queen's R W Surreys, who won his award for an action on 21 March 1918 at Le Verguier where he held on to his post under heavy fire until nearly all the garrison was killed. He was captured and died of wounds incurred on that day on 18 April 1918. Also buried here is **Capt the Hon Robert Bruce**, 34, 2nd ASH, 26 August 1914, 'Master of Burleigh' and **Capt Archibald Kennedy**, 2nd ASH, 26 August 1914, brother of Capt P. A. Kennedy, who has a Private Memorial (qv) in Fromelles.

This general area formed a focus for the attacks of the 7th (Ger) Division and from here the German artillery had clear views over the British positions.

Walk to the southern border of the cemetery.

The view to the south is directly towards the high ground of the le Cateau ridge beyond the town and over which runs the Roman road (a southern extension of the road you have just used) and on which 5th Division made its stand. Note the white water tower on your left. It is a useful reference point.

Return to the N43, turn left and continue into le Cateau, uphill past the splendid Matisse Museum on the left to the Mairie on the left with some parking.

On the *Mairie* wall is a list of citizens shot by the Germans, including seven who were executed for flouting the prohibition on keeping carrier pigeons [and there is a major memorial to the pigeons and a similar martyr in Lille]. Beside it is the **Tourist Information Office** where leaflets listing the town's hotels and restaurants may be obtained. Sadly the Hotel Mouton

Blanc, where the patronne hid several wounded British officers in August 1914, is no more.

During the Retreat Sir John French had his advance HQ in the *Mairie* at Bavay but visited le Cateau (where his main GHQ was situated) briefly on 24 August 1914 when he was gratified to see the leading elements of 4th Division. He then moved GHQ to St Quentin on the evening of the 25th.

Continue uphill and turn left on the N43 signed Toutes Directions. Continue to the first traffic lights at a crossroads.

N.B. To the right is the Rue du Marché aux Chevaux in which is the town Library. In it may be found one of the **British field guns (Map/5)** that took part in the 1914 action. By turning left at the end of the road is the Rue de Fesmy on which is the local Cemetery. Incorporated into it is the **British Le Cateau Communal Cemetery** which was used by the Germans to bury British dead in August and September 1914 and by the British in the last three months of 1918. In it there are some 150 burials including thirteen Australians. The Germans used le Cateau as a railhead and had a major hospital in the area. It is likely that the British had medical facilities here too as many of those buried in the cemetery died after the Armistice, including **Chaplain 4th Class Ernest Edward Johnson** on 1 December 1918.

Drive straight over and park as soon as you can. Walk back to the crossroads.

German grave marker, 26 August 1914.

- **66TH DIVISION COMMEMORATIVE HORSE TROUGH/6.9 MILES/5 MINUTES/MAP/4**

At the corner on the right as you walk back is a horse trough with a plaque in memory of the members of the 66th Division of the BEF who 'fell in the liberation of le Cateau from German occupation in October 1918'. The town was entered late on 10 October 1918, after four years of occupation, by the 5th Connaught Rangers.

Return to your car and continue on the N43 under the Cambrai-Ors railway and through Bazuel. Just before the Poilu Memorial fork left on the D160A to Ors. Turn left on the D160B following green CWGC signs to Ors Communal Cemetery. Stop at the local cemetery on the right. Walk through the local graves to the hedge-enclosed CWGC plot at the rear.

- **GRAVE OF WILFRED OWEN, ORS COMMUNAL CEMETERY/11.5 MILES/15 MINUTES/MAP A/1**

In the back row is a headstone inscribed '**Lieutenant W.E.S. Owen, MC,** Manchester Regiment, 4th November 1918. Age 25.' A somewhat reluctant soldier – he didn't join up (in the Artists' Rifles) until 15 October 1915 – Owen was commissioned in the Manchester Regiment on 4 June 1916. He arrived in France in January 1917 and saw action near Serre on the Somme. In March he was concussed but rejoined his battalion in April at Savy where he was shell-shocked. Then followed the famous episode at Craiglockhart War Hospital near Edinburgh where he met Siegfried Sasson and Robert Graves and wrote some of his most searing war poetry. He rejoined the 5th Manchesters in November and the following month was promoted to full Lieutenant. In August 1918 he arrived at Etaples and subsequently rejoined the Manchesters at Amiens. For his part in an action at Beaurevoir-Fonsomme Owen was awarded the MC. The reluctant soldier had become a fine regimental officer. In October his battalion took over the line west of the Sambre-Oise Canal and by 2 November they had cleared the west bank at Ors of the last enemy. Owen was detailed to lead his company in the dangerous canal crossing by raft with orders that there should be 'no retirement under any circumstances'.

66th Division Commemorative Horse Trough, le Cateau.

Headstones of Lt Wilfred Owen, VC and 2nd Lt James Kirk, VC, Ors Comm CWGC Cemetery.

Detail of Plaque.

WFA Plaque to Crossing of the Sambre-Oise Canal.

At 0545 on 4 November the Manchesters pressed on despite murderous fire from the heavily defended German bank. At 0700 hours, under swirling mist and gas, the attack was aborted. Among the dead were Owen, **2nd Lt James Kirk** and **A/Lt Col John Neville Marshall, CO** of the nearby Lancashires. Both the latter were awarded the **VC** for their gallantry and cool leadership during the costly crossing and their graves are in the same row as Owen's.

In one of the war's tragic ironies, his beloved mother, Susan, received the telegram informing the family of his death as the Armistice bells were ringing in his home town of Shrewsbury.

Owen's short military career provided him with the material for the unforgettable poetry, such as *Anthem for Doomed Youth*, *Dulce et Decorum Est* and *Strange Meeting*, that make him probably the most read of all the Great War poets.

The D160B on which you are parked is a no-through road. Beyond in the forest is the old military camp (marked on local maps) where the Manchesters

71

gathered before the attack on the canal. At the far end of the forest, approached from the D959 le Cateau-Landrecies road, is the 'Forester's House'. On 31 October Owen wrote home from 'The Smoky Cellar of the Forester's House' an upbeat, but sadly ironic, letter, warmly and enthusiastically describing the camaraderie of the officers and their servants. 'It is a great life.... There is no danger here, or if any, it will be well over before you read these lines'. There are now plans by the local authorities to create a **Wilfred Owen Museum in the old Forester's House**. This will be part of an ambitious 'Cité de la créativité' cultural project for the site. For details contact the *Mairie* (Monsieur Duminy) at Ors, Tel: + (0)3 27 77 62.

Turn round, return to the main road and turn left into Ors, passing the Mairie on the right. Drive over the canal and park immediately on the right. Walk back over the bridge to the memorial on the left as you walk.

- **WILFRED OWEN WFA MEMORIAL, ORS/12.1 MILES/10 MINUTES/MAP A/2**

The handsome black WFA plaque was unveiled by the Chairman of the Wilfred Owen Association in 1991. It commemorates the crossing of the Sambre-Oise Canal by 32nd Division on 4 November 1918 during which four VCs were won and amongst whose casualties was the poet Wilfred Owen, killed on the towpath about one kilometre to the north of the bridge.

The surviving **VCs were Res Maj Arnold Horace Santo Waters (later Sir Arnold) and Sapper Adam Archibald.**

Return to your car and continue to the next turn to the right on the D360 signed Catillon/La Groise. Continue to the junction with the N43 and turn left signed La Groise. Follow signs to Guise and continue to the traffic lights. Turn sharp left on the D934 and stop immediately by the memorial on the right.

- **1ST DIVISION MEMORIAL/15.6 MILES/ 5 MINUTES/MAP A/3**

This handsome memorial was erected 'To the Glory of God and to the abiding memory of the 1st Division of the BEF which from August 1914 to November 1918 served and suffered in France and left there close upon 160,000 dead'. It bears the quotation 'Who [sic] stands if freedom fall, Who dies if England live?' from Rudyard Kipling's 1914 poem, *For All we Have and Are*. It shows the figure of St Michael.

A plaque bears the ORBAT of the Division and a further plaque records that the memorial was re-erected by 32nd Eng Regt and blessed in the presence of the Mayor and Citizens of La Groise and officers and Maj-Gen Alexander-Sinclair and men of the 1st Division based in Germany on 28 August 1977. At that time it was moved back from the roadside where it had been hit several times by passing cars. Since that time the memorial has been maintained by the CWGC for the MOD. It stands at the crossroads

where at noon on the 26 August 1914 the Division was first attacked and compelled to fall back and where on the morning of 4 November 1918 those crossroads formed the centre of its line of consolidation seven days before the Armistice. It is, therefore, rather like the 'First and Last Shots' memorials at Mons (qv). The original memorial was sculpted by R. Goulden in 1926 and cast by A.B. Burton. It was inaugurated on 17 April 1927 in the presence of Marshal Foch, Lt-Gen Sir Arthur Holland and Sir Peter Strickland.

Return to Catillon and continue on the N43, over the Sambre-Oise Canal and turn left to Maizinghien on the D160. At the crossroads in the town turn right on the D115 signed le Cateau.

1st Division Memorial, la Groise.

On the right is the local **Maizinghien cemetery with a green CWGC plaque (Map A/4)** on the wall. It contains a line of headstones from 4 November 1918, including 7 Loyal North Lancs buried shoulder to shoulder and 1 Unknown German from the same date.

Turn right on the D12 to le Cateau. Continue to the cemetery on the left. Stop and walk to the back wall of the cemetery.

- **HIGHLAND CWGC CEMETERY/24.3 MILES/ 15 MINUTES/MAP/6/OP**

At the back of the cemetery look right along the wall and just to the left on the skyline are two distinct poplar trees. This is the area of le Cateau Station where the first German attacks began. Left of the poplars is a line of trees and just on their left, as they end, the Suffolk Memorial may be visible on the skyline.

Further left is a factory complex which indicates, to a first approximation, the route of the valley of the Selle and left again a large single bushy-top tree on the skyline indicates the village of Reumont where 5th Division had its HQ. It is readily seen from here how the German 5th Division's advance from the railway station area up the Selle River Valley outflanked the Suffolk's position. The skyline running right to left is the route of the Roman road and indicates the line taken by the British 5th Division as it retired on the afternoon of 26 August.

Rudyard Kipling called these military cemeteries 'Silent Cities' and a look at a number of graves

Highland CWGC Cemetery, le Cateau.

here shows the diverse nature of some of them: **Pte Osborne**, an Australian, was wounded, commissioned, invalided out, rejoined and then killed; **Rfmn King**, a deacon, the son of a priest, who had to obtain his Bishop's permission to enlist; **Lt Skemp**, Professor of English at Bristol University; **Pte Supple**, a 19-year-old boy; **Pte Torgerson**, an American from Minnesota.

The cemetery was begun by the 50th (Northumbrian) Division in October 1918 and the name comes either from the high ground on which the cemetery stands or the 32 graves of the Black Watch that are contained within it. Altogether there are some 620 burials.

Continue towards le Cateau under the railway bridge.

To the left is the le Cateau Railway Station.

Continue to the traffic lights and go straight over on the D21 following signs downhill to J. Rostand College to the main road and turn left on the N43. Continue uphill to the traffic lights and turn left, still following signs to the College. Continue past the hospital on the right and bear left and then right until you reach the College. Just before it is a bumpy track to the right. This can be negotiated by car if dry (if wet 4-wheel-drive would be advisable) and you have good ground clearance. Keep to the right at the fork at the top of the hill and continue to the memorial in the clump of trees.

- **THE SUFFOLK MEMORIAL/26.6 MILES/ 15 MINUTES/MAP/3**

You are now on the high ground of Point 139. This marks the centre of the Suffolks' position, one of the four infantry regiments that made up 14th Brigade, part of 5th Division. The other regiments were the 1st East Surreys, the 1st Duke of Cornwall's Light Infantry and the 2nd Manchester Regiment.

The original II Corps order issued from Corps HQ at 2215 hours on 25 August, just over an hour after Sir John French's withdrawal order arrived, envisaged the retreat continuing on 26 August and early that morning the Suffolks had already started to withdraw when, at 0600 hours in thick morning mist, they were stopped and told to hold the spur. Half of the Brigade did not receive that order and were in the skirmish action near the railway station. The Suffolks, therefore, had no choice of position and had to scratch shallow trenches where they stood, taking up thin firing lines on the forward slope of the feature you have just climbed and facing in an arc generally to the north and north-east.

The supporting artillery, 11th, 52nd and 37th (Heavy) batteries of 15th Brigade Royal Field Artillery (RFA), was lined up some 200 yards behind the Suffolk's trenches but in front of reserve troops so that the guns were actually sited among the infantry. As you can see the position is totally exposed. The only camouflage available to the gunners were stooks of corn which they lashed to the gun wheels.

By facing north you can see the white water tower referred to at the International Cemetery, and to the east the skyline marks the high ground beyond the valley of the River Selle, ground that the Germans occupied very early in the morning and thus opened II Corps' right flank. The initial forward movement of von Kluck's forces was towards you from the right of the tower as you look at it and German forces worked their way south along the valley of the River Selle. German machine guns were sited in the area of the tower.

Lt Col Stevens commanding 15th Brigade RFA told 52nd Battery, 'We will fight it out here and there will be no retirement', and before the guns could be properly dug in they came under rifle fire. Soon after 0600 hours

German artillery opened up causing considerable casualties among the gunners and the drop-shorts fell on the Suffolks in their shallow trenches.

At about 1000 hours a German infantry attack began to develop from the area of the River Selle (see **Map 3** for orientation) just south of le Cateau and 52nd Battery inflicted considerable damage on the enemy despite having several limbers set on fire by a German HE shell. Another infantry attack began at noon from the ground left and inclusive of the white water tower. Once again it was discouraged by the artillery. The gunners' fire controller had his OP well forward in the front line of the Suffolk trenches and his instructions to the guns were relayed back by a chain of orderlies lying out in the open because all telephone wires had been destroyed.

The volume of noise beating down on the trenches was horrendous. German HE shells from some one hundred guns were bursting overhead and our own guns, between 100 and 200 yards away, added their own cacophony as they returned fire.

Despite attempts at reinforcement by the Manchesters and Argyll and Sutherland Highlanders, the courageous tenacity of the gunners and the steady markmanship of the Suffolks, the German effort built up steadily against this flank, moving ever closer and at mid-morning an aerial observer reported that a 6-mile long column of German infantry was moving down the Roman road towards the crossroads (near the International Cemetery which you visited earlier).

As targets appeared the artillery engaged them but, of the four British batteries supporting the positions on the ridge, only one remained intact at the end of the morning and most of the ammunition in the lines had been used. The 52nd Battery fired over 1,100 rounds in the action. At 1330 hours a message was received ordering the guns to withdraw, but heavy casualties among the horses, let alone both men and guns, made this no easy task.

'One of the saddest things I have seen was the wounded horses trying to keep themselves on their legs by leaning against the stooks of corn', said one Sapper officer.

Lt Col. Stevens who had earlier told 52nd Battery that there would be 'no retirement' (the word 'retreat' had not yet come into use in the BEF) decided that he needed confirmation of the order to withdraw before acting upon it and it was not until 1400 hours that the guns of the Brigade were told to move. There was no escape for the 52nd, however, because their CO, Major A. C. R. Nutt, did not receive any order at all.

German infantry were attacking to the right of the Suffolks and working clear round them. A hail of machine gun fire poured down from the guns near the water tower. The British field guns fired singly as best as they could, most of the men being dead or wounded, and the last minutes were described by Lt Col Stevens as follows:

'About 2.40 pm some cheering was heard on our right about 300 yards away and over the crest. About five minutes afterwards we heard 'Stand Fast' and 'Cease Fire' sounded and whistles blown. Then it was shouted down the line from the right, 'You are firing on friends'. All firing stopped at once. On standing upright and looking just over the crest we found everyone standing up and the firing line being rounded up by Germans. The position was lost, considerable numbers of the enemy being round our right and right rear.'

The fight had lasted eight hours. The memorial, a cenotaph, commemorates the actions of the Suffolks, the Manchesters, the Argylls and the supporting batteries of the Royal Artillery. It bears the names of the Officers, NCOs and Soldiers who were casualties of those regiments on 26 August 1914, many of whom are buried in the International Cemetery, such as Capt the Hon Bruce (Master of Burleigh), 2nd ASH. There are 3 Drummer Boys: L. C. Hill, D. Yeatsley and A. Offley.

Return to the traffic lights on the main road and turn left on the N43 to Cambrai. Continue to the junction with the D932 below the International Cemetery (27.9 miles).

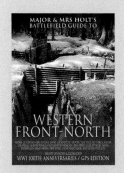

MAJOR & MRS HOLT'S BATTLEFIELD GUIDES

'Invaluable in the field'– The Daily Telegraph

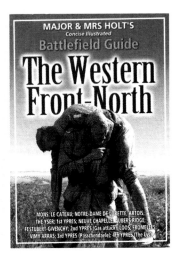

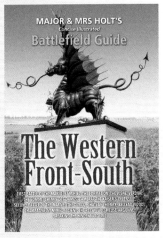

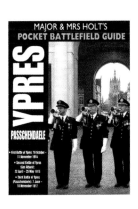

HOLTS' CONCISE ILLUSTRATED BATTLEFIELD GUIDE - THE WESTERN FRONT NORTH

This book contains many fascinating but little-visited areas by travellers. Each battlefield starts with some pertinent quotations by participants, has a succinct Summary of the Battle, Opening Moves and What Happened sections then a Battlefield Tour which follows the same tried and tested formula as the rest of the series of a timed and measured itinerary with historic and anecdotal information at each stop.

ISBN: **0850529336** • Price: £15.99 • Paperback

HOLTS' CONCISE ILLUSTRATED BATTLEFIELD GUIDE - THE WESTERN FRONT SOUTH

This book contains many fascinating but little-visited areas by travellers. Many of them have lain virtually 'dormant' for many years (such as areas of the Meuse-Argonne and Champagne) but have recently been renovated and opened up by dedicated local enthusiasts. There are many 'gems' in store in this book. Each battlefield starts with some pertinent quotations by participants, has a succinct Summary of the Battle, Opening Moves and What Happened sections then a Battlefield Tour which follows the same tried and tested formula as the rest of the series of a timed and measured itinerary with historic and anecdotal information at each stop.

ISBN: **1844152391** • Price: £15.99 • Paperback

MAJOR AND MRS HOLT'S BATTLEFIELD GUIDE TO YPRES SALIENT

This is the most complete guide to the First World War Battlefield of Ypres that has ever been published. There are recommended timed itineraries and every stop on the routes has an accompanying description and often a tale of heroic or tragic action. Memorials large and small, private and official, sites of memorable conflict, the resting places of personalities of note - they are all here and joined together by a sympathetic and understanding commentary that gives the reader a sensitivity toward the events of 1914-1918 that can only be matched by visiting the battlefield itself.
INCLUDES FULL COLOUR FOLD-OUT MAP WORTH £3.99
ISBN: **0850525519** • Price: £14.95 • Paperback

HOLTS' POCKET BATTLEFIELD GUIDE TO YPRES AND PASSCHENDAELE

Covering the important WW1 Battles of Ypres, including the notorious Passchendaele, this guidebook takes readers on a historic trip through some of the well-known and most important sites of the area. This book is designed conveniently in a small size, for those who have only limited time to visit, or who are simply interested in an introduction to the historic battlefields, whether on the ground or from an armchair. They contain selections from the Holts' more detailed guides of the most popular and accessible sites plus handy tourist information, capturing the essential features of the Battles. The book contains many full colour maps and photographs and detailed instructions on what to see and where to visit.

ISBN: **1844153770** • Price: £6.99 • Paperback

ORDER NOW!

Tel: 01226 734222 • **www.pen-and-sword.co.uk**

PEN AND SWORD BOOKS LTD, 47 CHURCH STREET, BARNSLEY, SOUTH YORKSHIRE S70 2AS.

THE FIRST BATTLE OF AISNE AND THE FIRST BATTLE OF YPRES

The First Battle of the Aisne was the Allied follow-up offensive against the right wing of the German First Army (led by Alexander von Kluck) and the Second Army (led by Karl von Bülow) as they retreated after the First Battle of the Marne earlier in September 1914. The offensive began on the evening of 13 September, after a hasty pursuit of the Germans.

By William Langford

Extracted from *The Great War Illustrated: 1914* and reproduced by permission of Pen & Sword Books Ltd.

When the Germans turned to face the pursuing Allies on 13 September, they held one of the most formidable positions on the Western Front. Between Compiègne and Berry-au-Bac, the Aisne River winds westward and is about one hundred feet wide, ranging from twelve to fifteen feet deep. Low-lying ground extends a mile on each side, rising abruptly to a line of steep cliffs three to four hundred feet high, then gently leveling to a plateau. The Germans settled on the higher northern side two miles (3 km) beyond the crest, behind a dense thicket that covered the front and slope. Low crops in the unfenced countryside offered no natural concealment to the Allies. Deep, narrow paths cut into the escarpment at right angles, exposed any infiltrators to extreme hazard. The forces on the northern plateau commanded a wide field of fire.

It soon became clear that neither side could budge the other and since neither chose to retreat, the impasse hardened into stalemate that would lock the antagonists into a relatively narrow strip for the next four years.

The First Battle of Ypres, also called the First Battle of Flanders, was a First World War battle fought for the strategically important town of Ypres in western Belgium in October and November 1914. The German and Western Allied attempts to secure the town from enemy occupation included a series of further battles in and around the West Flanders Belgian municipality.

The strategy of both the Allied and German armies is not entirely clear. The accepted and mainstream reasoning for the Ypres battle was the British desire to secure the English Channel ports and the British Army's supply lines; Ypres was the last major obstacle to the German advance on Boulogne-sur-Mer and Calais. The French strategy was to prevent German forces from outflanking the Allied front from the north. This was the last major German option, after their defeats at the First Battle of the Aisne and First Battle of the Marne. The Ypres campaign became the culmination of the Race to the Sea. The opposing armies engaged in offensive operations until a big German offensive in mid-October, which forced the Allies onto the strategic defensive and limited to counter-attacks.

The battle highlighted problems in command and control for both sides, with each side missing opportunities to obtain a decisive victory. The Germans in particular overestimated the numbers and strength of the Allied defences at Ypres and called off their last offensive too early. The battle was also significant as it witnessed the destruction of the highly experienced and trained British regular army. Having suffered enormous losses for its small size, "The Old Contemptibles" disappeared, to be replaced by fresh reserves which eventually turned into a mass conscripted army to match its allies and enemies. The result was a victory for the Allies, although losses were particularly heavy on both sides. The battle completed the entrenchments of the "race to the sea" and inaugurated the static western front. Mobile operations would not resume until 1918.

British artillery position on the Aisne.

Tommy arrives by civilian transport and receives a warm welcome in this French town.

British occupying the town of Braisne where heavy fighting took place in this street. The Germans fired from the houses where they had waited to ambush the pursuing Allies.

The French town of Soissons, situated by the River Aisne, was the scene of heavy fighting. It was here that British troops crossed the river.

A road leading to the Allies' positions during the fighting on the Aisne showing halted French transport.

British infantry dug in to slit trenches and dug-outs on the Aisne.

Parallel with and on both sides of the River Aisne the opposing armies dug in and an intense period of shelling began. The German had their heavy artillery in quarries behind the ridge and, supported by field guns, they poured a rain of shells onto the British and French positions.

Machine gun position of the 1st Cameronians in the front line at St Marguerite, 24 September 1914, during the fighting either side of the Aisne river.

German infantry manning shallow trenches.

The French have dug a mass grave to bury around 300 dead Germans. They appear to be using quick lime spread over the corpses and covering over with earth as the trench is being filled.

British shelters connected to the trench system on the Aisne. The beginnings of what would later become more permanent dwellings for the duration of the war over the next four years.

German officers' dugout: shelters would become ever more elaborate once the war of movement had come to an end by December 1914.

German heavy howitzer in search of a target.

A French soldier stands guard at the door of the heavily damaged Rheims cathedral.

Indian and English soldiers buying drinks before setting off on a series of attempts to outflank the German line along the Aisne. The Tommy with the six years Good Conduct Stripes is also wearing a Gun-layer's badge above them.

Mon of the 59th Field Company Royal Engineers ready to move out.

The Germans also were seeking an open flank to turn. German scouts watering their horses in a French village.

A French sniper. Note the bayonet, for his Lebel rifle, nicknamed 'Rosalie'.

How the first bombs were dropped. Crewman of Royal Naval Flying Corps takes aim.

British aviators receive instructions before taking off to locate the latest German positions as the opposing armies race to out-flank each other.

British infantry marching north towards Ypres.

83

A British heavy artillery column.

Marketplace of Thielt, north east of Ypres, Belgium. The 2nd Battalion Scots Guards filling the square, 12 October 1914.

2nd Battalion Scots Guards digging trenches near Ghent 9 October.

British cavalry arrives in the square at Ypres 13 October 1914. A defensive salient would form around this Belgian town and it would be fought over for the next four years. The buildings shown here would be reduced to piles of rubble.

Taking up firing positions across a road near Ypres, these men of the 2nd Royal Scots Fusiliers prepare to stop the German advance.

Another building wrecked in the same bombardment as the above. An eyewitness account dated 16 November 1914 reads: As each successive attempt to take Ypres by assault fails, the bombardment of the unhappy town is renewed with increasing fury.

German artillery.

The Cloth Hall, Ypres during the early bombardment. The tower proved to be an ideal aiming point for the German artillery.

British troops leaving a French town and returning to their units after recovering from illnesses, accidents or slight wounds.

Very welcome letters from home being distributed to men of the 19th Infantry Brigade at a roadside farmhouse during the First Battle of Ypres, October 1914.

Men of the 2nd Scots Guards arriving at billets in Zillebeke after being relieved by French troops in the Ypres Salient.

British transport wagons on the Menin Road during the First Battle of Ypres.

British soldiers await the attacking Germans.

German infantry in mid bayonet charge.

German machine gun crew operating a Maxim 08.

Men of the 2nd Battalion Scots Guards behind the lines at Ypres, October 1914.

Men of the London Scottish grab a bite to eat on a French railway station.

A few of the London Scottish, survivors of the fighting, marching off to billets near Bailleul, via La Clytte.

Indian troops arrived in France in October and were fully committed in December.

Germans among the sand dunes tending a comrade's grave.

After the Battle of Messines. With minimal training at the front; without maps; with mal-functioning rifles and without the support of their machine guns the Territorial battalion had met a superior number of the enemy and stopped its advance on Ypres.

The roll call near Wolvergham after the Battle of Messines. Only 150 officers and men answered. In the days that followed stragglers turned up and finally it was accounted that 394 officers and men had been killed or were missing.

November 11: The Germans finally ceased in their attempts to capture Ypres until the following year – April 1915.

Sergeants of the London Scottish rest during their march towards Wytschaete.

London buses used to transport troops to the front. These are men of the 2nd Battalion, the Warwickshire Regiment.

German Uhlan, dismounted and engaging the enemy with rifle fire.

London Scottish at their morning ablutions in a French town.

London Scottish in their 'skirts' which arouse curiosity. Upon arriving in France the battalion was dispersed and was employed on line-of-communica-tion duties throughout northern France. The men here, working on overhead telegraph wires, have decided to suspend their activities for some reason.

Men of the Ox and Bucks Light Infantry behind the lines at Ypres.

Awaiting the enemy.

Machine gun section guarding a road.

Germans observing the effects of the fighting.

German infantrymen strike a pose for the camera.

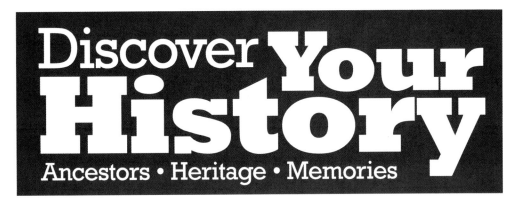

'Their shrapnel is bursting 600 yards in our rear around the steeple of the village church. I distinctly heard the clock on the church tower chime the hour of nine. It was the last nine it ever chimed as it went 'bang' with the next salvo of shells.'

A MOST PECULIAR CHRISTMAS

It would not be appropriate to end this examination of the British and German armies in the battles of 1914 without discussion of the remarkable series of spontaneous – and never again repeated – truces that broke out in certain points of the line on Christmas Eve and Christmas Day. It may be tempting to think of the fighting dying away after the First Battle of Ypres and as Christmas approached, but in fact the Truce is all the more remarkable when one considers the fact that there was heavy fighting in some sectors right up to Christmas Eve.

By Matthew Richardson

Extracted from *1914 Voices from the Battlefields* and reproduced by permission of Pen & Sword Books Ltd.

From the Ypres salient, an anonymous Bavarian soldier wrote home to Landshut on 26 December to describe the events of the previous day. Only one Bavarian regiment participated in the truce in this area, the Bavarian *Reserve Infanterie Regiment Nr. 17* which faced the men of the BEF at Kemmel, thus allowing us to locate the events that he describes quite closely:

> I must straight away recount to you what occurred yesterday on Christmas Day in the part of the line held by our regiment. It was Christmas Eve and we sang 'Silent Night, Holy Night' in our fire trench, which in places is only 40, 50, 90, 100 and at most 150 metres distant from the English. After we had finished singing the English applauded, and afterwards sang also, at which we applauded; then an Englishman came out of the trench, waved and shouted 'Hurrah!' Others went further, and also shouted 'Hurrah!' across. One of our men, who spoke English, shouted back and then he went across without his rifle. We followed him, and we and the English reached out to shake hands. Many had a very pleasant time. We exchanged cigars, cigarettes, gloves whatever one had, with each other. Afterwards, until two in the afternoon, there was no shooting. During the day it happened that first one came out, then several; finally there stood together a group of 40 to 50. One Englishman even gave one of us a haircut. At New Year they intended to meet us again, if we were in the line. However we have now been relieved and are having three days rest ...

By this stage in the war, more British Territorial formations were beginning to take their place in the line, alongside Regular battalions. Private E.R.M. Fryer served with one of the first such units to reach France, the Honourable Artillery Company, and he was also in the line in the Kemmel sector, opposite the Bavarians. He remembered a gloomy yuletide:

> We had Christmas Day in the front line, a thick fog making things even pleasanter. We dropped our plum puddings in the mud, and altogether it was very dismal. However, the Boche was very quiet, and we had no shelling at all, so we were thankful for small mercies. This Kemmel had been the scene of a bloodsome conflict between the French and the Boche, and the dead still lay thick on the ground; there was one particularly nasty group of Frenchmen caught by some wire and mown down.

Private Alfred Pollard was with the same unit, and provides a more detailed description of the events here at Kemmel:

> We spent Christmas Day in the front line. At midnight on Christmas Eve we sang all the carols we could remember; the whole company in one huge chorus. After we had exhausted our repertoire there was a lull. Then the Bavarians started in their trenches. Christmas Day was uneventful. There was no shelling and both sides were unusually quiet. At noon [we] decided to let Fritz know we were on the alert and contemptuous of him. We climbed on to the fire-step and fired off five rounds rapid. There was no reply. Christmas dinner consisted of bully beef and biscuits and Christmas pudding. The pudding was supplied by the kindness of the Daily Express. They were in tins, one between three men. We got a cup of hot tea to wash it down. The cold was intense; the ground was in the grip of a hard frost.

Slightly further south was another Territorial battalion, the 1st/6th Cheshires. One of its members gave an account of events here, the animals present attributable to the fact that before the war came to this part of Belgium only a few weeks previously, it had been farming country:

No Man's Land, where we fraternized. We ate their Sauerkaut, and they our chocolate, cakes, etc. We had killed a pig just behind our lines. There were quite a lot of creatures rambling about the lines, including an old sow with a litter and lots of cattle and poultry. We cooked the pig in No Man's Land, sharing it with the Boche. We also buried several dead Frenchmen who were lying out there. So ended our first Christmas in the line.

Private Joseph Killey of the 2nd Battalion Lancashire Fusiliers in a letter to his brother wrote of the truce near Ploegsteert Wood, not far away. Clearly the gifts from home were as important at this time of year as was the respite from warfare:

But as for fighting we have done nothing worth talking of since Xmas Eve but we might get a dam [sic] warm time yet like we had about a forenight [sic] ago ... thank your lucky stars you are at home and not out here for on Xmas

Captain E.M. Crawley-Boevey, Royal Sussex Regiment, attached 4th Battalion Royal Fusiliers, killed in action near Bailleul on 24 December 1914.

Soon after daylight arrived someone in our lines began to play 'Christians, awake!' on a mouth organ, and the thoughts of the men in the trenches immediately turned to the folks at home, who they knew were living under better conditions than they were. It was, says one who was there, nothing but mud, mud, mud, a parapet and two strands of wire between us and the Boche, who was 200 yards away. After 'Christians, awake!' the Boche responded with the popular melody 'Come over here!' and lo! we saw the Boche coming out of his trenches and we wondered whether it was an attack. The Germans were waving their arms, and immediately our men went out to meet them in

Private Albert Victor Read, of the 1st/6th Battalion Cheshire Regiment. This battalion was one of the first Territorial units to arrive in France, and Read was with it when it participated in the Christmas Truce south of Kemmel.

Private Joseph Killey of the 2nd Battalion Lancashire Fusiliers; he wrote home: 'on Xmas Day ... was not a shot fired worth talking about'. (Courtesy of Manx National Heritage)

Eve and night some of our poor chaps were near frozen to the ground as they were up to there [sic] knees in water & mud and on Xmas Day the [sic] was not a shot fired worth talking about for were [sic] we are I have heard them say that we have to wait a bit as we a [sic] to [sic] far ahead and we have to let the Lancs get up to make advance along the line when they get up. Well Ned the RFA has done a big share of the fighting up heare [sic] as it is all duels very near only a bit of sniping at night time when we relieve one another in the trenches which is 4 days in and 4 days out. We are out for the New Years Day but we were in all Xmas and I got Lillies card and pipe & tobacco which I was very thankful to her for sending them.

No clearer contrast between the social classes of enlisted man and officer in the BEF could be provided than that demonstrated by Killey's testimony and that of Lieutenant J.C.W. Francis of the 19th Hussars. This unit provided the divisional cavalry of the 4th Division, in the southern part of the British line near Ypres. Though apparently not in the front line at Christmas, Francis never the less recorded his approval of the events of which he was aware in a diary entry:

> *Christmas Day: What a wonderful day no cannons going off no rifles, nothing, absolute peace. I have now quite forgotten there is a war going on at all, one goes about wishing people happy Christmas everybody looks merry and bright and bar a wagon or two one might be in the most peaceful part of Europe. Everybody seems to have stopped doing anything as if by mutual consent too busy thinking about their plum puddings etc I suppose but it is perfectly ripping.*

Further south, Private H.A.Taylor of the 1st Battalion Cameronians, was in the line near Armentières. He remembered many years later the details of events and also a special memento:

The opposing lines were so close one could hear the Boche singing carols, they were Bavarians. Not a shot was fired during Xmas eve or Christmas Day and on Boxing Day only a sniper was having potshots, but no casualties were reported. On Xmas eve a corporal and I escorted the rations up the line, we made the usual distributions to companies including the rum issue and found that we still had a jar of rum left, we gave our drivers a good issue and sent them back to our lines. We sat, of all places, outside the cemetery of Houplines having a tot or two, listening to the singing of the troops. It was a beautiful night moonlit and serene. We heard someone approaching, it turned out to be our new Regimental Sergeant Major, he enquired what we were doing there, we explained that we were listening to the singing. We offered him our jar of rum, meantime I told him his batman had drawn his issue, by the time

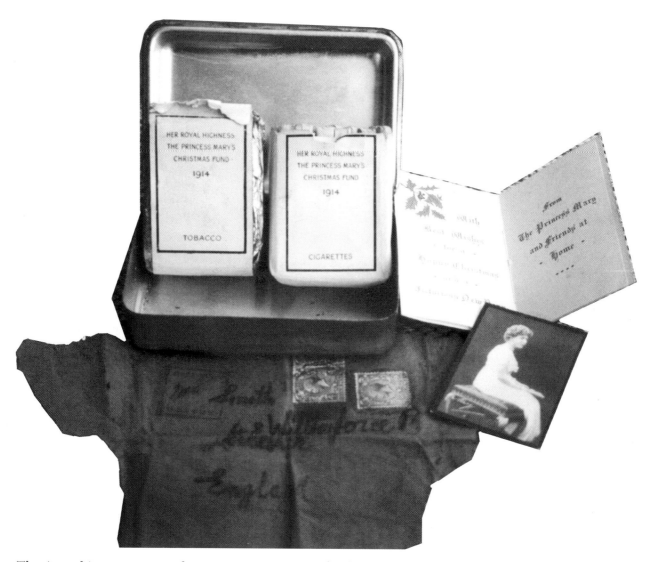

The tin and its contents sent by HRH Princess Mary's fund to soldiers in France at Christmas 1914. This example belonged to Private Bernard Smith of the 1st Battalion Leicestershire Regiment, who sent it home to his mother in Leicester.

he left we were all merry, wishing us a Merry Xmas he made his way to Headquarters and we strolled back to billets, which was a large school building. Our Quarter Master was surprised when told of the singing etc. after two hours rest we were ordered to Steenwerck our rail-head to collect the Princess Mary's gift box to the British Expeditionary Force. It was an ornamented brass box, bearing the portrait of her and allied flags, containing cigarettes and tobacco. Everyone received his box, even those in hospital and next of kin of those killed of my regiment had one sent to them. I still have mine, polished and in a prominent place.

At the railhead were three trucks loaded with large bundles of gifts for Scottish troops at the front, just that, no specific regiment being mentioned. Our Q.M. Seargeant marked twenty of these bundles, '1st Batt. The Cameronians BEF' and ordered us to load them on our G.S. waggon. Inside them, after opening, were everything from shaving soap to socks, balaclava caps, sweets and a host of other things including cigarettes and plenty of well wishing notes from the donors, [and] many a romance commenced through these innocent notes.

Possibly the freely available rum had a worse effect on some than on others. Captain R.C. Money was in the same battalion and recalled that while there was no fraternisation, one soldier decided upon his own impromptu Christmas celebration:

So far as I know the only unrecorded incident was that one of our jocks, who had seen the rum rather too frequently, paraded down No Mans land, being cheered by the Germans, and an officer in the Royal Welsh Fusiliers whose front he had got onto by this time requested him to come in, and Jock replied, in terms that Jock was wont to use, that if he was wanted he could come and fetch him! It did lead to trouble in due course for the poor man, when he was sobered up!

Private Frank Richards was serving with the neighbouring battalion, the 2nd Royal Welsh Fusiliers, and although he does not confirm the incident with the drunken Cameronian, he none the less has provided a detailed account of events from the point of view of his battalion. He wrote:

On Christmas morning we stuck up a board with 'A Merry Christmas' on it. The enemy had stuck up a similar one. Platoons would sometimes go out for twenty-four hours rest – it was a day at least out of the trench and relieved the monotony a bit – and my platoon had gone out in this way the night before, but a few of us stayed behind to see what would happen. Two of our men then threw their equipment off and jumped on the parapet with their hands above

their heads. Two of the Germans done the same and commenced to walk up the river bank, our two men going to meet them. They met and shook hands and then we all got out of the trench. [An officer] rushed into the trench and endeavoured to prevent it, but he was too late; the whole of the company were now out, and so were the Germans. He had to accept the situation, so soon he and the other company officers climbed out too. We and the Germans met in the middle of no-man's-land. Their officers was also now out. Our officers exchanged greetings with them … We mucked in all day with one another. They were Saxons and some of them could speak English. By the look of them, their trenches were in as bad a state as our own. One of their men, speaking in English, mentioned that he had worked in Brighton for some years and that he was fed up to the neck with this damned war and would be glad when it was all over. We told him that he wasn't the only one that was fed up with it … The German Company-Commander asked [our officer] if he would accept a couple of barrels of beer and

A Christmas card sent home to his mother in the Leeman Road area of York by Private John Knott, King's Royal Rifle Corps, at Christmas 1914.

Bringing good cheer to the troops in France: the Royal Engineers Postal section, Christmas 1914.

assured him that they would not make his men drunk. He accepted the offer with thanks and a couple of their men rolled the barrels over and we took them into our trench ...

To the south, at L'Epinette, the line was held by the 1st Battalion Royal Fusiliers. A soldier serving with this battalion wrote of the truce in a letter to his sister. Tantalisingly the soldier is identified only as Ted, but on his part of the front the beer was going in the opposite direction:

On Christmas Eve, the Germans stopped firing, and our chaps did the same. No firing was done that night, and on Xmas Day our chaps, ready for sport, went over to the Germans and shook hands with them. We exchanged beer and cigarettes for wine and cigars, and one of the Germans cut off all his buttons and gave them to one of our men in exchange for a pair of puttees. Then we took a football over, and we were just going to play them a match when along came one of their fussy officers, three parts drunk, and raised Cain. He went off shocking, and ordered them back again, so we played ourselves, and they watched us and cheered. This is the truth, but as soon as 12 o'clock came, we started to fight again.

Alongside the Fusiliers in the British 6th Division, was the 1st Battalion Leicestershire Regiment, in the Rue du Bois district of the Armentières sector. Sergeant E.B. Hayball of this unit wrote:

Christmas Eve found the Battalion trenches covered with snow, and a brilliant moon lit

up No Mans Land and the enemy trenches. After dusk the sniping from the German trenches ceased and the enemy commenced to sing; their Christmas carol grew louder as their numerous troops in the reserve trenches joined in, and eventually ended with loud shouts and cheering. 'A' Company of our battalion then began a good old English carol, the regiments on right and left joining in also, and this was received by the enemy with cheers and shouts of 'Good! Good!' On Christmas Day snow fell heavily, and as the enemy did not snipe when the men exposed their heads, several of 'B' Company got out of their trench and stood upright in full view of the enemy; they were surprised to see the Germans do likewise, waving their hands and shouting in broken English ... At dusk the sentries manned the parapet as usual, but the enemy remained quiet ...*

In fact, Hayball is wrong in this last assertion as one man from this battalion was indeed sniped on Christmas Day. Lance Corporal George Sutton was shot and killed late on the afternoon of 25 December, his friend Private Bernard Smith was standing next to him at the time, and the tragic incident remained with him for the remainder of his days. At Christmas in later years he would recount to his daughter the story of how a German shouted a warning, but a shot followed all too quickly.

On the nearby Bois Grenier front, the Signals officer of 22nd Brigade Captain Richard O'Connor (later General Sir Richard O'Connor) was in the habit of visiting the units of his brigade in the front line each morning. He remembered his astonishment on one of his regular inspection visits to find a truce in full swing:

My Brigade was in the line ... and I went down on Christmas morning to the various units that I always used to go to and I saw it just start. I saw the enemy come over with white flags and then various people on our side walked out, and I amongst them, and we ... eventually came and talked to the Germans, and some agreement was arrived at about burying the dead; and I remember meeting one officer who was a German who said that he had been a member of the RAC but had been taken off it at the outbreak of war. However we went on. I stayed there a good deal of the morning and then went back and told the General about it ... some of his staff officers came out without red hats and had a look around and found out all there was to be found out and eventually we returned ...

After O'Connor had left, explicit instructions were issued to the front-line troops that the truce was to end

Private Bernard Smith (seated) and his friend Lance Corporal George Sutton, who was killed on Christmas Day.

forthwith, which it did, with both sides returning to their lines. As O'Connor noted, often the truce had a practical motive, that of providing a proper burial for the many corpses that littered no-man's-land. Lieutenant W.B.P. Spencer of the 2nd Battalion Wiltshire Regiment wrote to his mother on 28 December of just such a task:

Well here we are again after a very cold Xmas in the trenches. We went in on Xmas eve and saw about 9 or 10 lights along the German lines. These I said were Xmas trees and I happened to be right. There was no firing on either side during the night, which was one of very severe frost. On Xmas Day we heard the words 'Happy Christmas' being called out whereupon we wrote up on a board 'Gluchliches Weinachten' and stuck it up. There was no firing so by degrees each side began gradually showing more of themselves and then two of them came halfway over and called out for an officer. I went out and found that they were willing to have an

armistice for 4 hours and carry our dead men back halfway for us to bury. A few days previous we had had an attack with many losses. This I arranged and then – well you could never imagine such a thing. Both sides came out, met in the middle, shook hands, wished each other the compliments of the season and had a chat. This was a strange sight between two hostile sides, then they carried over the dead. I won't describe the sights which I saw and which I shall never forget. We buried the dead as they were, then back to the trenches with the feeling of hatred growing stronger after what we had seen. It was strange after just shaking hands and chatting with them. Well it was a very weird Xmas Day. There was very little firing during the two days.

Sergeant Jim Davey of the 2nd Field Company Royal Engineers, part of the same division, wrote in his diary of the opportunity that the Truce presented for defensive work:

Lieutenant W.B.P. Spencer, Wiltshire Regiment, wearing the British army's winter-issue goatskin coat. (Liddle Collection; reproduced with the permission of Leeds University Library)

[Christmas eve] Went out at 8pm with a sapping party to work all night. When we got in the trenches we found our infantry and the Germans out between the two lines talking to each other and exchanging things. Went over myself and exchanged p[laying] cards and cigarettes with a German officer. Being Xmas eve both sides in this quarter ceased firing by mutual understanding. Everyone walking on top of trenches so we did our job on top. Could hear them singing all night.

Boxing Day: Went to the trenches at 7.15am. Still no firing in our quarter everyone knocking about on top. Most peculiar Christmas I've ever spent and ever likely to. One could hardly believe the happenings. Bitterly cold all day & snowing slightly. Xmas pudding for dinner. Rum issue at night.

Captain R. Archer-Houblon was a Royal Horse Artillery Forward Observation Officer close by in the frontline trenches at La Boutillerie. He remembered taking the opportunity for exploration of no-man's-land:

I was still up in the trenches, but the Yorkshires had relieved the Bedfords on Christmas Eve. Christmas Eve was a clear bright frosty night, and all through the long evening hours the Germans had been very merry and singing all along the line. They had, too, a violin, a cornet, a flute and an accordion, and the strains of these, together with several men with remarkably good voices, could be heard in the still sharp air as clearly as if they had been but a few short yards away. While we were looking out over the parapet and listening to the concert, suddenly we became aware of a voice in No Man's Land calling out to us not to shoot, and proposing that someone should come out to discuss and arrange a truce to celebrate Christmas the following day. After some hesitation the company commander, a subaltern who knew a little German, went out to meet the emissary and, I think, finally agreed that if we could get permission we would put a flag on the parapet the next morning. Christmas morning was bitterly cold and dawned in a dense blinding fog; not twenty yards could be seen from the trenches, so, forgetting all about the proposal for a truce, I seized the opportunity to go out and explore the ruins of La Boutillerie. Then, somewhat later, I returned, when as I

A German newspaper exchanged in no-man's-land by Major R. Archer-Houblon for a copy of the Daily Mail, during the Christmas Truce.

approached our trench the mist began to rise, and presently to my astonishment disclosed a No Man's Land filled with numbers of unarmed Germans! They had not troubled to wait for a flag to appear on our parapet, but had flocked out of their trenches in the fog, and here was the truce in full swing, a 'fait accompli'! What was to be done? As a matter of fact, before anything could be done, everyone had climbed out into the open and had joined in the fun. It was of course not long before urgent messages began to come from in rear to put a stop to the proceedings; but though it was naturally frowned upon by the authorities, there was however no real harm in the truce. It was due simply to sheer curiosity. Many of us, even among those who had been out quite long, had never seen a hostile German at such close quarters before; and not only to see them close, but also to be able to examine every detail of their features and uniform, was a temptation no keen soldier could resist. In fact it was all most deeply interesting. They were, as far as I can remember, the 16th Prussians, and they looked very clean and bright, we thought, and like everyone else they said that they wished the war was over. One said that he had lived in Brighton, another that he had been to school in Birmingham, and a third, an officer, had lived most of his life in America – details lamentably dull now, but amazingly interesting when told us in No Man's Land by an enemy in time of war. I exchanged one of our newspapers for a German one, and the men dealt in all sorts of odds and ends.

In fact, Archer Houblon retained the copy of the *Täglichen Rundschau* which he had received in exchange for a copy of the *Daily Mail* for the rest of his life, a prized memento of one of the most extraordinary incidents in the history of warfare.

Second Lieutenant M.D. Kennedy of the 2nd Battalion Cameronians was in the line near Neuve Chapelle, where a truce was signalled by the Germans somewhat earlier than on other parts of the front:

With us it wasn't Christmas Eve, it was 23rd December. One of my men suddenly called out to me and said to me 'There are some Germans Sir, out there, they are getting out of their trench and waving to us!' Well I was wondering what to do about it, I had a look, they were obviously friendly, but I got an order from my company commander, 'Count the Germans, but on no account go out to meet them.' So that's what happened. This went on for most of that day. That evening we were relieved in the trenches, and while that was happening the Germans started singing Christmas carols. As far as my company was concerned there was no fraternising, but in the company on my left, they allowed two Germans to come over and they met in the middle.

This account seems to chime with that of Karl Aldag, a philosophy student at Marburg before the war, and now serving with one of the German reserve regiments. He was in the Fournes area, south of Armentières, and wrote to his parents:

Christmas at the Front! We were relieved on the evening of the 23rd around 10 o'clock. The

German soldiers unpack Christmas boxes sent from home, December 1914.

English had been singing hymns, including a fine quartet. On our side too the beautiful old songs resounded, with only now and then a shot in between. The sentry posts in the trenches were decorated with fir branches and tinsel from home, also the dug-outs ... it was the clearest, most beautiful night we have had for a long time, just as still and pure as Christmas ought to be. It was freezing too, which put an end to the mud and filth. I thought much about home ...

The line south of here was held by the Indian Corps, and Captain Alexander, of the Indian Mule Corps, remembered that the Sikh and Muslim soldiers under his command were also provided for with royal gifts:

The village in which our billets lay was called Burbure, and here we spent Christmas Day which was fine and frosty – one of the nicest days we had had for some time. In the morning Rennison and I paid a visit to the refilling point to exchange the season's greetings with our friends. There was a larger crop of presents than ever. Sergeant Grainge, the quartermaster, required extra carts to carry them away. Every man had a Christmas card from the King and Queen, with photographs of their Majesties. Princess Mary's present of an artistic box, containing a pipe, tobacco and a packet of cigarettes, was distributed to all ranks. From Queen Mary also each man received a pair of socks. All these were highly appreciated, and many announced that of course they would not wear the socks: they would be treasured for all time. After the distribution on parade of the royal presents, Ressaidar Amir Khan called for three cheers for the King and Queen, and three

German soldiers unpack Christmas boxes sent from home, December 1914.

more for the Badshahzadi (the Princess). These were given with great enthusiasm ... A turkey purchased in Bethune, and a plum-pudding from England made our Christmas dinner reminiscent of home.

It was a remarkable conclusion, to an extraordinary four months. Nothing like the Truce would be seen again in the ensuing four years of war, just as nothing like the battles of those four months would ever be seen again. Europe was on the cusp of history, turning away from battles waged by glittering cavalry and combat conducted like it was a summer exercise on Salisbury Plain or the Juteborg, towards an industrialised, impersonal form of war. Henceforth, men were to be just the fodder, fed into its voracious jaws.

The first five months of the Great War had borne witness to bitter fighting, with selfless heroism and bitter savagery abundant in equal measure. If the protagonists believed that the rule book of warfare had been torn up in the campaign of August to December 1914, little were they to know that this was just the curtain raiser for the next four years. If the men of the BEF were to overcome an enemy as numerous, resourceful and powerful as the Germans had proved

themselves to be in the battles from Mons to Ypres, it would require every ounce of resolve that they possessed. The final word in this goes to a British soldier writing home just before Christmas 1914. This man, Private Clement Ruscoe, had been in France since the initial landing of the Expeditionary Force in August. In his letter he told his former employer:

I think the Germans by this time will know that the British Tommy is a terrible being once he is properly aroused. The Germans have gone the proper way about things to fairly rouse our men, by their ferocious and wanton behaviour in Belgium, and there can be no turning back until the power for a repetition of this terrible work is forever taken out of their hands.

If, as many assert, the British Regular had arrived in France in August 1914 with a professional soldier's disinterest in who or what his enemy was and what he represented, then his direct first-hand experience of that enemy, and what he was capable of, bred in him a desire to smash German militarism once and for all. It was a conviction that would stay with and sustain the BEF through four brutal and bloody years on the Western Front.

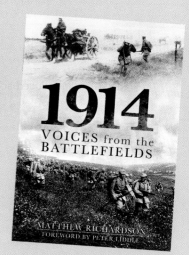

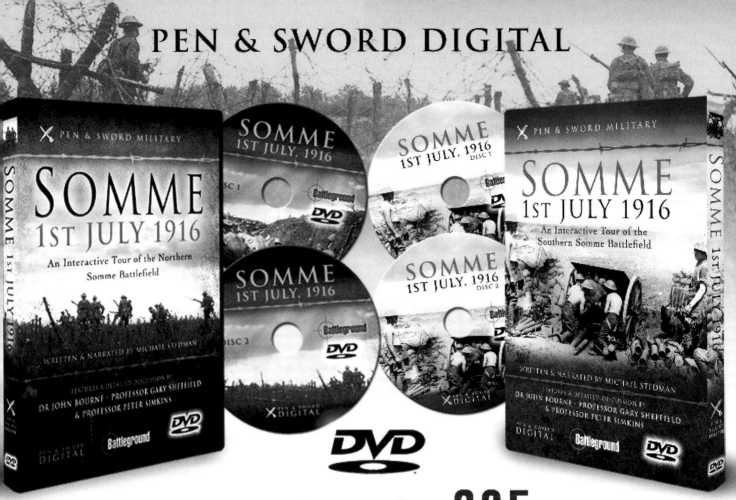

Pen and Sword have developed an unrivalled reputation for the quality and scope of its battlefield guides.

The series covers a whole range of battles right from the battle of 1066 up to the crucial battles of WW1 and WW2. Famous Great War battles include Anzio, Aisne, Cambrai, Mons, Gallipoli, Oppy Wood, Passchendaele, the Somme and Ypres.

These well written books, full of colourful and detailed illustrations not only bring the battlefields alive for tourists and vistors but they also inform and entertain readers at home. Using a distinctive blend of historical narrative and personal accounts supported by copious illustrations, these attractive and affordable books have a huge following.

For those looking to understand battles in a bit more detail, then the battleground series, now with over 100 titles in print, is perfect for the armchair historian or battlefield traveller alike.

 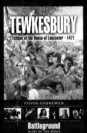   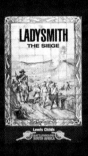 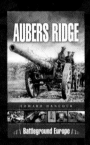  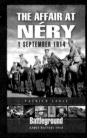
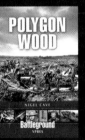  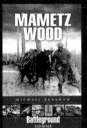 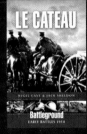   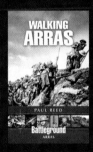 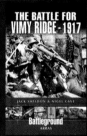
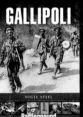     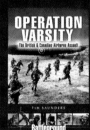  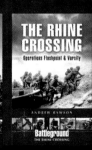
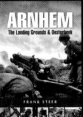 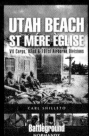  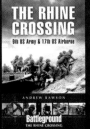 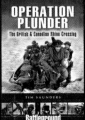 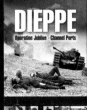  

'Heads were bobbing about and showing over their parapet in a most reckless way, and, as we looked, this phenomenon became more and more pronounced. A complete Boche figure suddenly appeared on the parapet, and looked about itself.'

BAIRNSFATHER'S CHRISTMAS TRUCE

Trench life was a great shock to Bairnsfather and he concealed his true feelings, as many officers did, under a puerile, public school approach to the war. It became a team game in which ritual patterns soon developed, so that preoccupation with routine dulled overt sensitivity to the horror all around.

By Tonie and Valmai Holt

Extracted from *In Search of the Better 'Ole* and reproduced by permission of Pen & Sword Books Ltd.

Christmas 1914 saw a lull in the 'game', and Bairnsfather took part in one of the most extraordinary episodes of the Great War, an episode that might have brought him a court martial. It started on Christmas Eve. He tells the story himself.

The day had been entirely free from shelling, and somehow we all felt that the Boches, too, wanted to be quiet. There was a kind of invisible, intangible feeling extending across the frozen swamp between the two lines, which said *'This is Christmas Eve for both of us – something in common.'*

About 10 pm I made my exit from the convivial dug-out on the left of our line and walked back to my own lair. On arriving at my own bit of trench I found several of the men standing about, and all very cheerful. There was a good bit of singing and talking going on, jokes and jibes on our curious Christmas Eve, as contrasted with any former one, were thick in the air. One of my men turned to me and said:

'You can 'ear 'em quite plain, sir!'

"Hear what?" I inquired.

'The Germans over there, sir; you can 'ear 'em singin' and playin' on a band or somethin'.

I listened; away out across the field, among the dark shadows beyond, I could hear the murmur of voices, and an occasional burst of some unintelligible song would come floating out on the frosty air. The singing seemed to be the loudest and most distinct a bit to our right. I popped into my dug-out and found the platoon commander.

'Do you hear the Boches kicking up that racket over there?' I said. 'Yes,' he replied: *'they've been at it some time!'* 'Come on,' said I, *'let's go along the trench to the hedge there on the right – that's the nearest point to them, over there.'*

So we stumbled along our now hard, frosted ditch, and scrambling up on to the bank above, strode across the field to our next bit of trench on the right. Everyone was listening. An improvised Boche band was playing a precarious version of *Deutschland, Deutschland, über*

Alles, at the conclusion of which, some of our mouth-organ experts retaliated with snatches of ragtime songs and imitations of the German tune. Suddenly we heard a confused shouting from the other side. We all stopped to listen. The shout came again. A voice in the darkness shouted in English, with a strong German accent, *'Come over here!'* A ripple of mirth swept along our trench, followed by a rude outburst of mouth organs and laughter. Presently, in a lull, one of our sergeants repeated the request, *'Come over here!'*

'You come half-way – I come half-way,' floated out of the darkness.

Bruce Bairnsfather.

113

Bainsfather captures the Christmas Truce in this cartoon.

Lieutenant Bainsfather on his way to the Christmas Truce, December 1914, St Yvon.

'*Come on, then!*' shouted the sergeant. '*I'm coming along the hedge!*'

'*Ah! but there are two of you,*' came back the voice from the other side.

Well, anyway, after much suspicious shouting and jocular derision from both sides, our sergeant went along the hedge which ran at right-angles to the two lines of trenches. He was quickly out of sight; but, as we all listened in breathless silence, we soon heard a spasmodic conversation taking place out there in the darkness.

Presently, the sergeant returned. He had with him a few German cigars and cigarettes which he had exchanged for a couple of Maconochie's and a tin of Capstan, which he had taken with him. The seance was over, but it had given just the requisite touch to our Christmas Eve – something a little human and out of the ordinary routine.

After months of vindictive sniping and shelling, this little episode came as an invigorating tonic, and a welcome relief to the daily monotony of antagonism. It did not lessen our ardour or determination; but just put a little human punctuation mark in our lives of cold and humid hate. Just on the right day too – Christmas Eve! But, as a curious episode, this was nothing in comparison to our experience on the following day.

On Christmas morning I awoke very early, and emerged from my dug-out in the trench. It was a perfect day. A beautiful, cloudless blue sky. The ground hard and white, fading off towards the wood in a thin low-lying mist. It was such a day as is invariably depicted by artists on Christmas cards – the ideal Christmas Day of fiction.

Walking about the trench a little later, discussing the curious affair of the night before, we suddenly became

'Well, if you knows of a better 'ole, go to it'

aware of the fact that we were seeing a lot of evidence of Germans. Heads were bobbing about and showing over their parapet in a most reckless way, and, as we looked, this phenomenon became more and more pronounced.

A complete Boche figure suddenly appeared on the parapet, and looked about itself. This complaint became infectious. It didn't take 'Our Bert' long to be up on the skyline (it is one long grind to ever keep him off it). This was the signal for more Boche anatomy to be disclosed, and this was replied to by all our Alf's and Bill's, until, in less time than it takes to tell, half a dozen or so of each of the belligerents were outside their trenches and were advancing towards each other in no-man's land.

A strange sight, truly!

I clambered up and over our parapet, and moved out across the field to look. Clad in the muddy suit of khaki and wearing a sheepskin coat and Balaclava helmet, I joined the throng about half-way across to the German trenches.

It all felt most curious: here were these sausage-eating wretches, who had elected to start this infernal European fracas, and in so doing had brought us all into the same muddy pickle as themselves.

This was my first real sight of them at close quarters. Here they were – the actual, practical soldiers of the German army. There was not an atom of hate on either side that day; and yet, on our side, not for a moment was the will to war and the will to beat them relaxed. It was just like the interval between the rounds in a friendly boxing match. The difference in type between our men and theirs was very marked. There was no contrasting the spirit of the two parties. Our men, in their scratch costumes of dirty, muddy khaki, with their various assorted head-dresses of woollen helmets, mufflers and battered hats, were a light-hearted, open humorous collection as opposed to the sombre demeanour and stolid appearance of the Huns in their grey-green faded uniforms, top boots, and pork-pie hats.

The shortest effect I can give of the impression I had was that our men, superior, broadminded, more frank, and lovable beings, were regarding these faded, unimaginative products of perverted culture as a set of objectionable but amusing lunatics whose heads had got to be eventually smacked.

> 'I clambered up and over our parapet, and moved out across the field to look. Clad in the muddy suit of khaki and wearing a sheepskin coat and Balaclava helmet, I joined the throng about half-way across to the German trenches.'

British and German soldiers nervous of the photographer in case of repercussions.

'*Look at that one over there, Bill,*' our Bert would say, as he pointed out some particularly curious member of the party.

I strolled about amongst them all, and sucked in as many impressions as I could. Two or three of the Boches seemed to be particularly interested in me, and after they had walked round me once or twice with sullen curiosity stamped on their faces, one came up and said '*Offizier?*' I nodded my head, which means 'Yes' in most languages, and, besides, I can't talk German.

These devils, I could see, all wanted to be friendly; but none of them possessed the open, frank geniality of our men. However, everyone was talking and laughing, and souvenir hunting.

I spotted a German officer, some sort of lieutenant I should think, and being a bit of a collector, I intimated to him that I had taken a fancy to some of his buttons.

We both said things to each other which neither understood, and agreed to do a swap. I brought out my wire clippers and with a few deft snips, removed a couple of his buttons and put them in my pocket. I then gave him two of mine in exchange.

Whilst this was going on a babbling of guttural ejaculations emanating from one of the *laager-schifters*, told me that some idea had occurred to someone.

Suddenly, one of the Boches ran back to his trench and presently reappeared with a large camera. I posed in a mixed group for several photographs, and have ever since wished I had fixed up some arrangement for

Bairnsfather with time on his hands in the winter of 1914 .

On the edge of Ploegsteert Wood at Le Gheer. It was on ruined buildings in this area that Bruce Bairnsfather began his cartooning.

getting a copy. No doubt framed editions of this photograph are reposing on some Hun mantelpieces, showing clearly and unmistakably to admiring strafers how a group of perfidious English surrendered unconditionally on Christmas Day to the brave Deutschers.

Bairnsfather at work – one of his own cartoons.

"My Dream for years to come

Young inquisitive replacement: "Who made that 'ole?" Fed-up old soldier: "Mice!" The Germans felt the need to explain this when they used it in a manual on humour. 'It was not mice. It was a shell.'

Slowly the meeting began to disperse; a sort of feeling that the authorities on both sides were not very enthusiastic about this fraternizing seemed to creep across the gathering. We parted, but there was a distinct and friendly understanding that Christmas Day would be left to finish in tranquillity. The last I saw of this little affair was a vision of one of my machine-gunners, who was a bit of an amateur hairdresser in civil life, cutting the unnaturally long hair of a docile Boche, who was patiently kneeling on the ground whilst the automatic clippers crept up the back of his neck.

The Commander of the BEF, General Sir John French, heard about the Christmas Truce, as it became known, and although in retrospect his attitude mellowed, at the time he reacted firmly:

'I issued immediate orders to prevent any recurrence of such conduct and called the local commanders to strict account...'